PITTSBURGH STEPS

The Story of the City's Public Stairways

BOB REGAN

photos by Jeff Wingard

Globe Pequot

Guilford, Connecticut

The cover painting is *Middle Street*, an acrylic by Pittsburgh artist and steps enthusiast Cynthia Cooley (cynthiacooley.com). Thank you, Cynthia.

Globe
Pequot

An imprint of Rowman & Littlefield

Distributed by NATIONAL BOOK NETWORK

Copyright © 2015 by Bob Regan
All photos © 2015 Jeff Wingard

British Library Cataloguing in Publication Information available

Library of Congress Cataloging-in-Publication Data available

ISBN 978-1-4930-1384-5 (paperback)
ISBN 978-1-4930-1385-2 (electronic)

∞™ The paper used in this publication meets the minimum requirements of American National Standard for Information Sciences—Permanence of Paper for Printed Library Materials, ANSI/NISO Z39.48-1992.

*This work is formally dedicated to all of
Pittsburgh's city steps enthusiasts and supporters—
the people who appreciate, enjoy, and
work to preserve these unique assets.*

*Informally we dedicate this work to Jeff's sons,
my grandsons Zack and Brian.*

CONTENTS

Figures

Acknowledgments

In our quest to publicize and save Pittsburgh's city steps there are many people and organizations worthy of acknowledgment. Here we highlight a few, but offer thanks to all.

Jed Lyons, president and CEO of Rowman and Littlefield, is responsible for the existence of this book after immediately grasping the significance of the city steps from an article in the *Wall Street Journal.* From the start of our quest and throughout the years, Diana Nelson Jones, reporter for the *Pittsburgh Post-Gazette*, has tirelessly championed the steps in print. The cleaning of many sets of steps has been made possible through a generous grant from the Leon Falk Family Trust.

To these and many others, Pittsburgh's city steps offer a profound *thank you!*

PREFACE

My previous book, *The Steps of Pittsburgh,* was published in 2004. For the first time, these unique and wondrous assets of Pittsburgh were accurately assessed and documented by means of detailed mapping and descriptions and through the dramatic, artistic photography of Tim Fabian. That book generated a great deal of publicity for the city and since then hundreds of people from around the world have visited the city to explore the steps.

The attention brought to the city steps was certainly rewarding. An equal but more personal reward was a letter I received from noted author and historian David McCullough, a Pittsburgh native. Mr. McCullough wrote, in part, "I am absolutely delighted to have your wonderful *The Steps of Pittsburgh.* What an inspired idea! And I can't tell you how many memories it brings back to this old son of the city. The pictures are a feast unto themselves."

Unfortunately, the original book is long out of print and now available only through various resale markets. However, there still exists a demand for information on the city steps. After a decade I thought it timely to revisit these amazing features, not only to satisfy such a demand, but also to update the state of the city steps in 2015.

In this visit to the city steps I was fortunate to be able to utilize the wonderful photography of Jeff Wingard of Creative Imagery LLC who casts a different light on the subject matter.

Introduction

Many cities have major rivers to contend with, while others are challenged by hilly terrain. Pittsburgh is fairly unique in that it battles both. Within the confines of its 50 square miles, the city hosts three major rivers as well as numerous hills, valleys, and runs (known as creeks or streams to the rest of the world). The central portion of the Pittsburgh is located at the confluence of the Allegheny and Monongahela Rivers where they form the Ohio River. This "Three Rivers" location is well known as the name of the city's former professional sports stadium. Abutting the flat river areas are rather steep, winding hills and valleys that were sculptured from the Allegheny Plateau.

Indeed, geologically speaking there is no other city in the world like Pittsburgh. Although there are many noted hilly cities, such as San Francisco, none of those hills developed for the reason that the hills in Pittsburgh did. Pittsburgh's topography is the result of the pure erosion, primarily due to the outflow of glaciers, of the stable 250-million-year-old Allegheny Plateau. There has been no major tectonic or volcanic activity or interruption of the local rock beds, only erosion.

The mix of rivers, hills, and valleys has proven to be both beneficial and problematic to Pittsburgh. It has been beneficial in that it has resulted in the city having much green space. Approximately 40 percent of the city is unsuitable for development. Additionally, topography is and has been a dominant factor in shaping urban development and delineating neighborhood boundaries. Indeed, it is so significant that it was the subject of a book entitled *The Spectator and the Topographic City*. The author, Martin Aurand, notes that ". . . Pittsburgh lies unevenly upon unruly land. Communities and neighborhoods are variously defined by hills and demarcated by hollows. . . . There are a great number and variety of contrivances for scaling, connecting, and otherwise negotiating the terrain, ranging from bridges to tunnels to inclined planes and public steps."

Thus, Pittsburgh is physiographically challenged. Its locale at the confluence of three rivers combined with the land's undulating terrain offers unique challenges to the development of transportation systems. The city has, however, risen to the challenge by combining unique modes of transportation with more conventional transportation solutions. The collection of transportation technologies includes city steps, inclines, trolleys, bridges, and tunnels.

Today Pittsburgh has more municipal inclines than any other US city and more city steps and bridges than any other city in the world. Additionally Pittsburgh had, at one time, one of the largest trolley systems in the country and its eleven transportation tunnels also rival, in number, those of most other cities.

Undoubtedly the city steps are the most unique of these transportation solutions. Pittsburgh has hundreds of streets complete with street signs, and oftentimes houses, composed entirely of steps. These "paper streets" are municipal rights-of-way and appear on many maps as valid thoroughfares, much to the consternation of unsuspecting motorists. Additionally, there are streets in Pittsburgh, uncomfortably steep for walking, that have steps for sidewalks. In addition to providing functional modes of transportation, the steps are dramatic and picturesque cultural features.

These steps are an integral part of the city's history and bear a relationship to the city's many diverse ethnic neighborhoods, another of Pittsburgh's most endearing features. Sixty-six of the city's ninety neighborhoods contain steps. Accordingly, the city steps can be seen as not only a result of the city's topography but also its rich cultural history.

City Steps

PITTSBURGH'S VARIATION IN TOPOGRAPHY HAS ALSO HAD A SOCIO-economic influence on the area. The flat land adjacent to the rivers, which were then a primary means of transport, was considered prime land for the area's many steel mills. Consequently, the only affordable, inhabitable land for the common people was on the hilltops or, in some cases, along the hillsides. In order for workers to travel to work, a series of steps were built to the steel mills. Originally the steps were privately built, but soon formal steps along rights-of-way were constructed by the municipality. The steps essentially became legal streets. These *city steps* were, in essence, the city's first mass transportation system. Subsequent to this primary need, city steps were also constructed throughout the city whenever steep topographic relief inhibited conventional street construction or to offer hilltop dwellers access to the lower environs.

The World Wide Web is alive with websites and blogs devoted to steps, stairs, and step and stair climbing. In such a context and for this study it is critical that the term *city steps* be defined. The Pittsburgh city steps are public stairways, owned and maintained by the City of Pittsburgh, located in public rights-of-way. This definition excludes steps in parks, privately owned stairways, and so forth. As such, this particular study was limited to the confines of Pittsburgh; these features are not limited to the confines of the city and exist elsewhere throughout the region.

The previous publication described 712 sets of city steps. Subsequent explorations have revealed a few dozen more sets of steps and the total number is now 739 sets of steps—a remarkable number in a city the size of Pittsburgh. Of these 739 sets of steps, 344 are legal streets. Conversely there are 344 streets in Pittsburgh that are nothing but flights of steps,

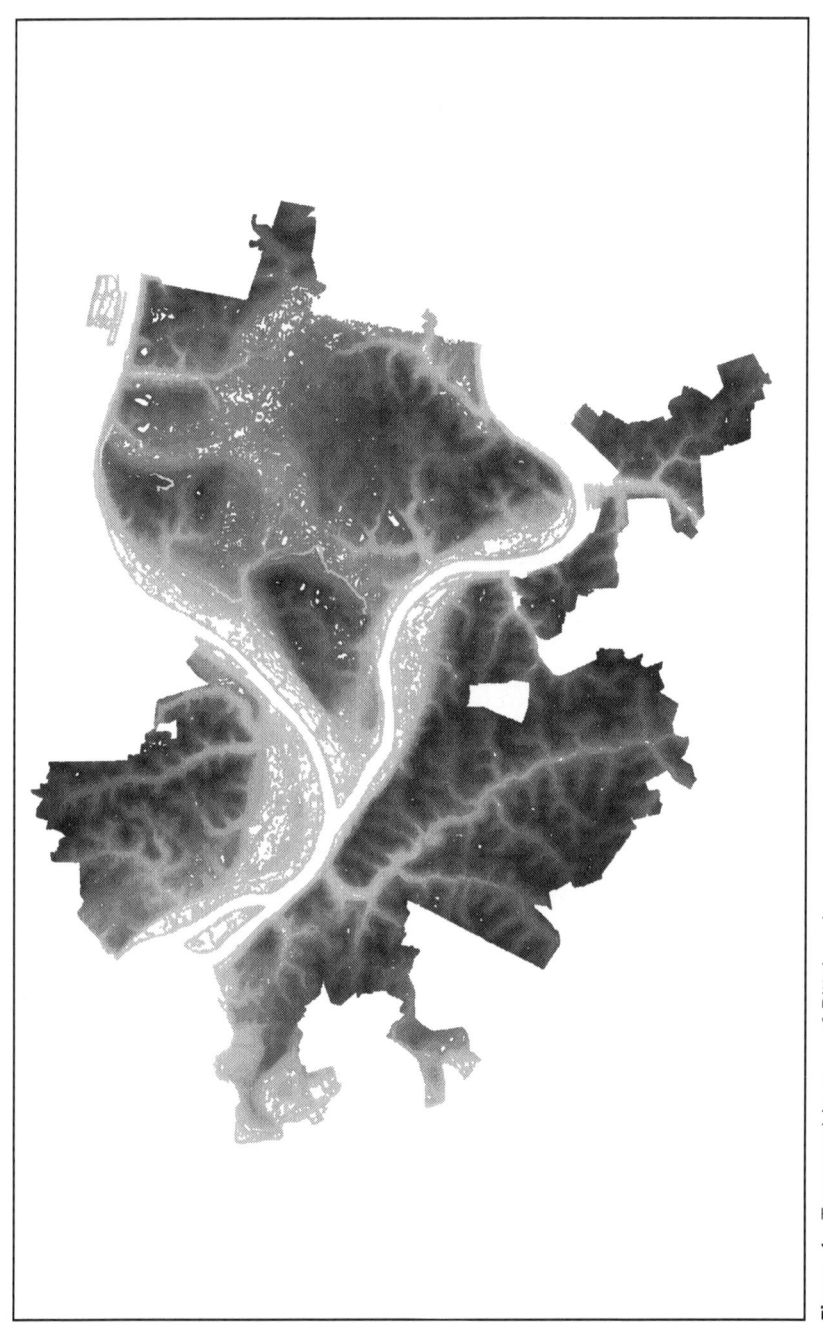

Figure 1. Topographic map of Pittsburgh

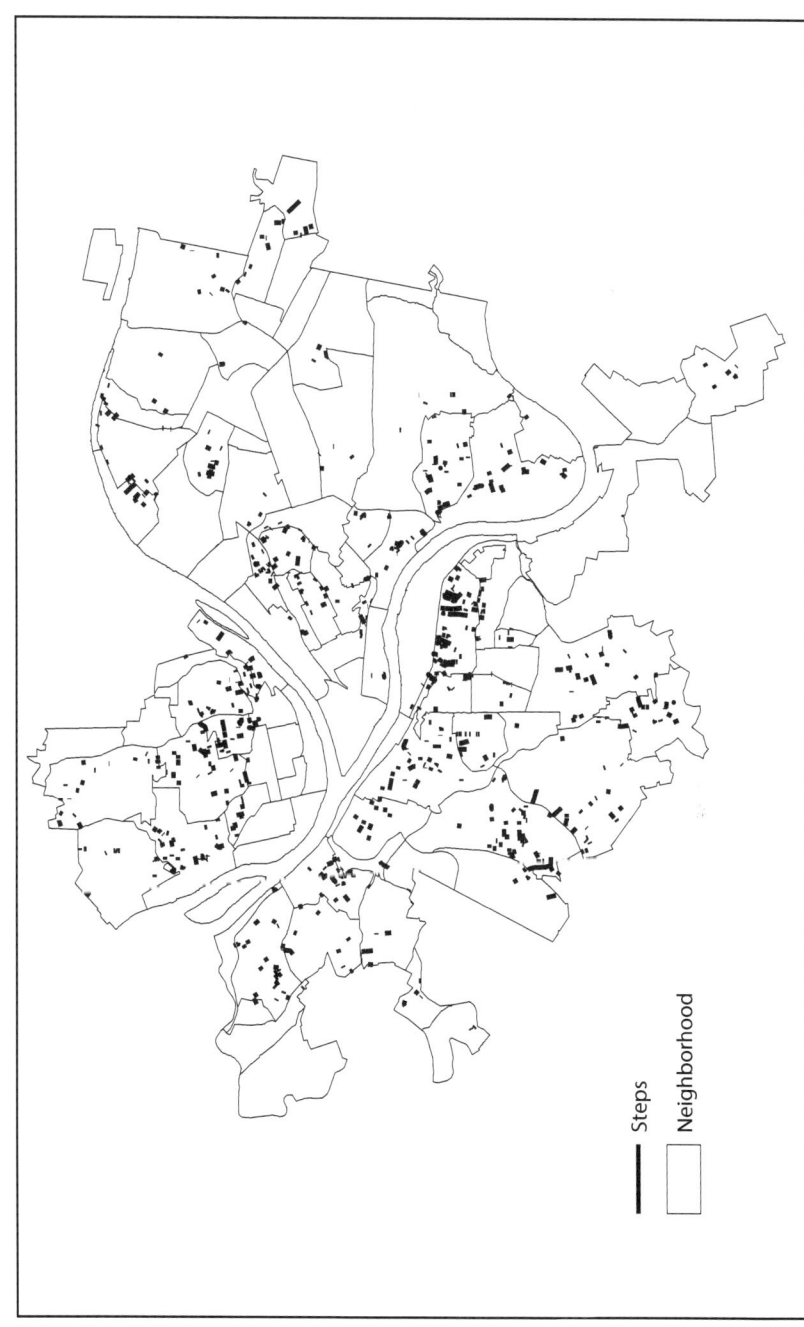

Figure 2. Map of locations of Pittsburgh's city steps

Steps

Neighborhood

Figure 3. View from the St. Thomas Street sidewalk steps

and 61 of these are wooden steps. Of the total number of sets of steps, 281 are sidewalk steps of which 30 are wood. The 739 sets of steps contain 45,454 steps, with each step being 0.54 feet in height. This leads to a total elevation change of 24,545.1 feet or 4.65 miles!

As noted, the fluvial and topographic obstacles have proven to be problematic to the development of suitable transportation systems. A hint of this can be gleaned from a topographic map such as the example shown in Figure 1. The change in elevation from the flats along the rivers to the irregular hilltops throughout the city is typically 200 to 300 feet with a maximum change of 600 feet.

A ground survey combined with sophisticated database and computer mapping techniques resulted in the detailing and mapping of 739 sets of city steps. Their distribution throughout the city, as shown in Figure 2, provides some hint of the topography of Pittsburgh. This is more apparent when Figure 2 is compared to Figure 1.

It is not practical or possible to provide a detailed mapping of the city steps in a publication such as this. However, ESRI, of Redlands, California, the company that produces the GIS software used in the mapping of the

Figure 4. James Street on the north side of Pittsburgh

Figure 5. Intersection of Ivondale and Anthony Streets

city steps, has graciously produced an interactive web mapping of them. Users can browse the locations of the city steps and click on a set of steps to obtain detailed information. ESRI has a close working relationship with the City of Pittsburgh and the city has agreed to host the website. The website's address is gis.pittsburghpa.gov/steps.

Additional information on the city steps is contained in Appendix A, which lists the locations of all 739 sets of steps as well as the number of steps in each set and the year they were constructed (if known).

However, mere words and numbers cannot do justice to these artifacts. They must be seen to be appreciated. A sampling of Pittsburgh's city steps is shown in Figures 3, 4, 5, and 6. As noted, 344 of the city steps are legal streets. One of the most dramatic is Diana Street in the Spring Garden neighborhood. Figure 7 shows a conventional paper road map indicating that one could drive on Homer Street and turn onto Diana Street. However what one encounters is shown in Figure 8. Indeed Diana Street is a dramatic set of high-rise steps, clearly not suitable for automobile travel.

Figure 6. Graib Street in the Fineview neighborhood

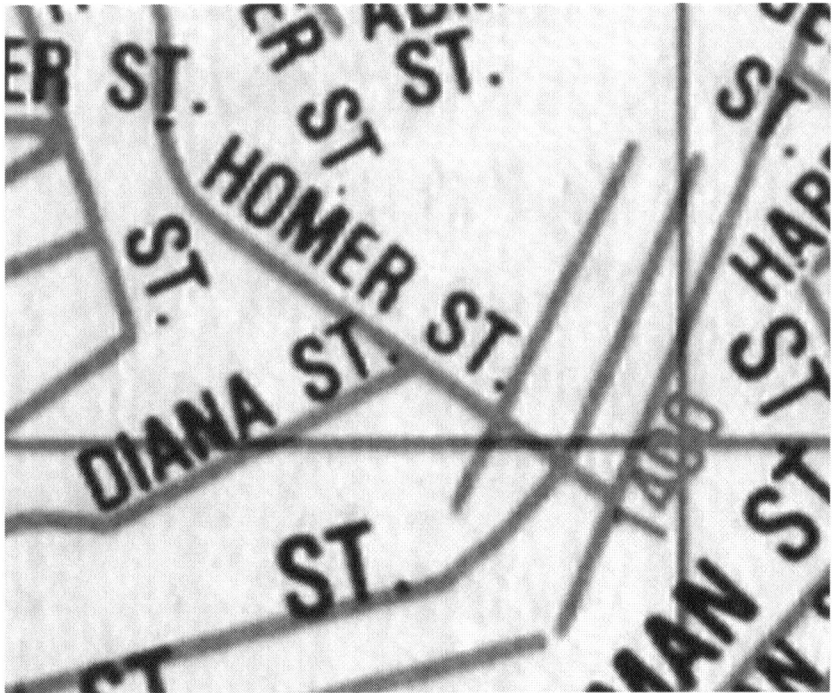

Figure 7. Section of road map showing Diana Street intersecting Homer Street

Perhaps the most intriguing set of street steps is in the Oakland neighborhood. Here two sets of street steps intersect on a secluded hillside. The intersection is adorned with a telephone pole complete with street light and street signs. Figure 9 shows the intersection of Frazier and Romeo Streets, while Figure 10 offers a dramatic view down Frazier Street. These street steps are used daily by neighbors and school children traveling to a bus stop. However, they are potentially threatened. The proposed Southern Beltway is slated to intersect with the Parkway East (I-376) at this locale. The planned interchange could destroy these unique artifacts. In 2005 I wrote to the Pennsylvania Turnpike Commission, builders of the Southern Beltway, the letter on page 12.

Figure 8. Diana Street at the intersection of Homer Street

Figure 9. Frazier/Romeo Streets intersection

Figure 10. Frazier Street in Oakland

Figure 11. Duncan Street where it transitions from a regular street into a set of wooden steps

Dear Mr. Brimmeier,

Re: Mon-Fayette Expressway Bates Street Interchange

I want to call attention to two sets of the City of Pittsburgh's public staircases that are located in the vicinity of the BATES STREET interchange.

The city has 737 sets of steps (more than any other city in the world), of which 342 are legal streets. Conversely, 342 of the city streets are composed solely of steps. The two streets composed of steps in the vicinity of the proposed interchange are the 60-year-old Frazier and Romeo St. steps. These are unique features in that the two streets (steps) intersect, complete with a telephone pole and street signs. I have enclosed a location map and photo.

I hope that in your design and construction of the interchange, you could preserve these unique historic features. Indeed, it would serve

Figure 12. Ardary Street in the Garfield Neighborhood

Figure 13. Homes on Gladstone Street in Greenfield

Figure 14. The single home on Dido Street

Figure 15. Upper 57th Street

Figure 16. Lower 57th Street

Figure 17. High-rise sidewalk steps at the intersection of Barry and Mission Streets

Figure 18. Inground sidewalk steps on Tunstall Street in Greenfield

the city well if you could incorporate them into your design, highlighting them, and welcoming all to America's "City of Steps."

Let us hope that reason, common sense, historic preservation, and civic pride prevail.

Lest we conclude that all street steps are large arrays of concrete steps, Figure 11 shows the wooden street steps that are a section of Duncan Street, in the Lawrenceville neighborhood. Another set of wooden street steps is shown in Figure 12. Clearly marked with a street sign, these are the Ardary Street steps in the Garfield neighborhood.

Although many street steps have no residences on them, a few do. Such houses, accessible only by the steps, are termed *orphans*. One resident of such an abode said, "You can forget about pizza delivery." Figures 13 and 14 show Gladstone and Dido Streets in the Greenfield neighborhood. These homes do have alternative means of access, while the homes along 57th Street in Lawrenceville are true orphans. Figures 15 and 16 illustrate this. These houses have mailboxes on the steps and also have steps themselves from the city steps to the house. There is no other access to the houses except via the steps. The thoughts that occur to a visitor are *Where do they park? What about groceries? What about moving?*

In addition to the many high-rise and street steps, there are also 281 sets of sidewalk steps, 22 of which contain more than 100 steps. The sidewalk steps are of two basic varieties—high-rise and in the ground. Examples are shown in Figures 17 and 18.

The City Steps with the Most Stairs

Raye Avenue	Brookline	378
Jacob Street	Brookline	364
57th Street	Stanton Heights	345
Rising Main Way	Fineview	331
Yard Way	South Side Slopes	317
Oakley Way	South Side Slopes	285
Eleanor Street	South Side Slopes	282

Steps in Various Neighborhoods

ANOTHER ALLURING ASPECT OF PITTSBURGH IS ITS MANY DIVERSE neighborhoods. Although there is no universal agreement on the number or names of all the neighborhoods, the Department of City Planning recognizes ninety neighborhoods, and their data was used to define the neighborhoods in the survey of the steps. As previously noted sixty-six of these ninety neighborhoods contain steps.

If one visits one of the hillside neighborhoods today, it is immediately apparent why the city steps are still a sensible means of transportation. The streets are quite narrow, often a car-and-a-half wide, and there is a continual ballet among the vehicles traversing the streets. It is worth noting that it is a quiet ballet, as no loud blaring of horns accompanies it. Residents are used to the dance, and the traffic moves haltingly but with a certain grace. One only wonders what transpires during one of the city's infamous winter storms. Yet this is when the steps are particularly useful. As one resident noted, "All the people in the area use the steps, particularly in the winter when the streets are slippery."

In addition to its neighborhoods, the city also has loosely divided geographic quadrants, termed in typical Pittsburgh fashion: the North Side, East End, South Side, and West End. To offer some additional insight into the steps, we highlight several locales in each quadrant of the city. In addition the interactive steps website gis.pittsburghpa.gov/steps can be used to examine steps in the various neighborhoods.

First, it is worth noting that the neighborhoods with the greatest number of sets of steps are as follows: South Side Slopes (68), Beechview (40), Mount Washington (35), Marshall-Shadeland (29), Brookline (29), Perry South (27), Greenfield (26), and Shaeraden (23). The steps in all the neighborhoods are summarized in Table 1, which details the number of steps by neighborhood throughout Pittsburgh.

NORTH SIDE

The North Side is that section of the city north of the Allegheny and Ohio Rivers, formerly known as Allegheny City. Incorporated into the City of Pittsburgh in 1907, this area is well known to sports fans as the former location of Three Rivers Stadium and now Heinz Field and PNC Park.

Although this is one of the hilliest sections of the city and contains the highest point of elevation (1,370 feet), there are only 157 sets of steps. This is undoubtedly due to the fact that there is no steep topography abutting the river banks except for the area near Troy Hill. Although there were no steel mills in this particular area, there were stockyards, tanneries, and meatpacking plants, not to mention the H.J. Heinz Company along the shore of the Allegheny River.

There are two neighborhoods on the North Side that contain a number of interesting and historic steps worthy of mention.

Fineview, formerly Nunnery Hill, is an aptly named neighborhood, as this area on a hillside north of Allegheny General Hospital offers one of the area's finest views of downtown Pittsburgh. Fineview has long appreciated the city steps in its locale. Indeed, this neighborhood hosts an annual Step-a-Thon, one of the most difficult 5K races anywhere, as its course traverses many of the city steps of this neighborhood. From its beginning, the Step-a-Thon was held to create awareness for the need to preserve the city steps and raise the funds to do so.

A map of the seventeen sets of city steps in the Fineview neighborhood is shown in Figure 19. Almost all of the city steps in this neighborhood are street steps. One of the most spectacular set of city steps in this neighborhood is Rising Main Way (Figure 20). This set of 331 steps rises from the valley to Fineview. The steps begin at the intersection of Toboggan Street (also a set of sidewalk steps), which, when viewed from the bottom, seems aptly named. Not far from Rising Main Way are several sets of street steps. An example is the Middle Street steps shown in Figure 21.

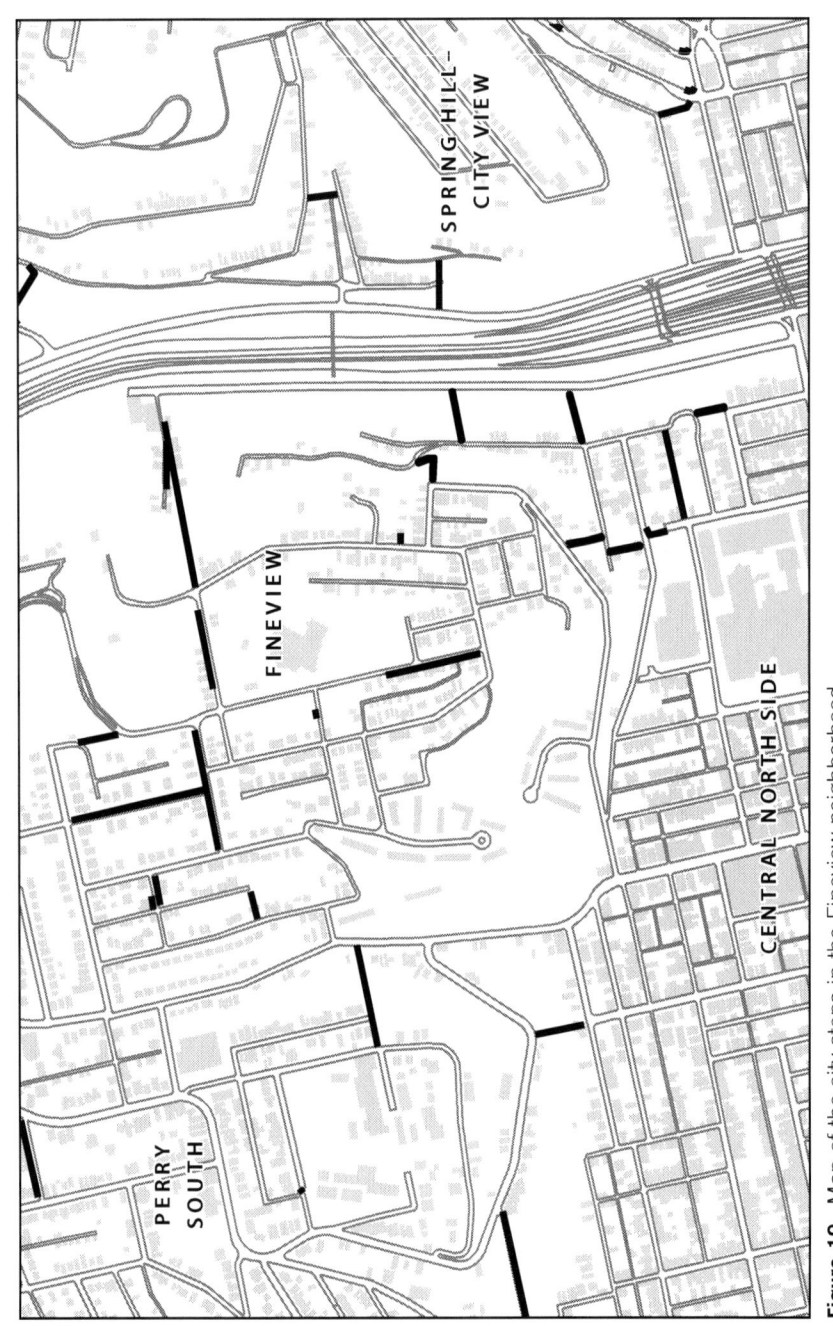

Figure 19. Map of the city steps in the Fineview neighborhood

Figure 20. The Rising Main Way Steps

Figure 21. View at the top of the Middle Street Steps

Figure 22. Rialto Street

Troy Hill is an old German neighborhood atop one of the steepest hills in Pittsburgh, actually an elongated plateau that parallels the Allegheny River near Herr's Island, now known as Washington's Landing. The quaint neighborhood appears almost removed from the rest of the city, being relatively isolated with only a few access roads.

Today, there is only one road, Rialto Street, complete with sidewalk steps (Figure 22), which leads directly from the banks of the Allegheny River to the Troy Hill neighborhood. Its twenty-four-degree slope ranks it as the fifth steepest street in the city. In addition to Rialto Street, there are two sets of city steps traversing this slope with only one set still accessible. The still functional set of steps is unnamed but connects East Ohio Street to Troy Hill Road at Goettman Street. The other, long abandoned, was Heckleman Street, which offered another access route from East Ohio Street to the top of Troy Hill (at Eggers Street). From 1887 to 1898, people had an optional means of transportation via the Troy Hill Incline located several hundred feet south of present day Rialto Street.

The backside of Troy Hill has several sets of steps leading up from the Spring Garden neighborhood. A particularly interesting flight is Harpster

Figure 23. Harpster Street

Street, as it has homes on it and an intersection with another set of city steps (Purse Way). These are shown in Figure 23.

Table 1. Steps by Neighborhood

NEIGHBORHOOD	SETS	TOTAL	MIN	MAX
1. Allegheny Center		no steps		
2. Allegheny West		no steps		
3. Allentown	11	433	7	100
4. Arlington	13	438	0	103
5. Arlington Heights		no steps		
6. Banksville	5	412	73	98
7. Bedford Dwellings	3	294	13	115
8. Beechview	40	2609	0	158
9. Beltzhoover	16	595	6	120
10. Bloomfield	4	161	14	97
11. Bluff	2	188	18	170
12. Bon Air	1	57	57	57
13. Brighton Heights	11	487	4	71
14. Brookline	29	1823	5	378
15. California-Kirkbride	9	748	19	209
16. Carrick	22	1146	8	167
17. Central Business		no steps		
18. Lawrenceville	1	9	9	9
19. Central Northside	4	395	62	140
20. Central Oakland	7	462	19	136
21. Chartiers City	2	131	81	81
22. Chateau		no steps		
23. Crafton Heights	9	632	12	117
24. Crawford-Roberts	3	88	25	35
25. Duquesne Heights	14	575	8	96
26. East Allegheny	4	352	11	143
27. East Carnegie		no steps		
28. East Hills	5	738	31	273
29. East Liberty				
30. Elliott	20	1560	3	232
31. Esplen	1	22	22	22

NEIGHBORHOOD	SETS	TOTAL	MIN	MAX
32. Fairywood		no steps		
33. Fineview	17	1350	7	331
34. Friendship		no steps		
35. Garfield	13	962	7	180
36. Glen Hazel	1	108	108	108
37. Greenfield	26	1445	2	251
38. Hays		no steps		
39. Hazelwood	18	1373	12	259
40. Highland Park	3	66	21	23
41. Homewood North	8	565	6	173
42. Homewood South		no steps		
43. Homewood West		no steps		
44. Knoxville	7	172	2	51
45. Larimer	2	93	0	93
46. Lincoln Place	5	248	18	77
47. Lincoln-Lemington	8	585	21	142
48. Lower Lawrenceville		no steps		
49. Manchester		no steps		
50. Marshall-Shadeland	29	1382	3	125
51. Middle Hill	9	441	12	106
52. Morningside	8	376	2	137
53. Mount Washington	35	1460	5	136
54. Mount Oliver	5	155	14	41
55. New Homestead		no steps		
56. North Oakland	4	72	7	28
57. North Shore		no steps		
58. Northview Heights		no steps		
59. Oakwood	6	57	11	28
60. Overbrook	15	921	8	221
61. Perry North	21	1163	3	168
62. Perry South	27	1709	0	232
63. Point Breeze	4	156	27	57
64. Point Breeze North		no steps		
65. Polish Hill	16	988	0	163
66. Regent Square		no steps		
67. Ridgemont	2	76	12	64

NEIGHBORHOOD	SETS	TOTAL	MIN	MAX
68. Shadyside		no steps		
69. Sheraden	23	1242	4	138
70. South Oakland	11	689	8	277
71. South Shore		no steps		
72. Southside Flats	2	83	27	56
73. Southside Slopes	68	5447	0	295
74. Spring Garden	12	865	4	192
75. Spring Hill-City V.	17	1419	4	254
76. Squirrel Hill North	4	252	4	98
77. Squirrel Hill South	7	150	4	39
78. Saint Clair	1	26	26	26
79. Stanton Heights	9	1050	47	345
80. Strip District	1	65	65	65
81. Summer Hill		no steps		
82. Swisshelm Park		no steps		
83. Terrace Village	3	157	50	56
84. Troy Hill	11	775	0	188
85. Upper Hill	15	695	4	126
86. Upper Lawrenceville	10	784	8	249
87. West End	4	79	0	42
88. West Oakland	7	485	5	157
89. Westwood	9	490	18	115
90. Windgap		no steps		

EAST END

The East End contains a diverse collection of neighborhoods rich in differing economic, ethnic, cultural, and racial backgrounds. In the midst of the area is one of the most international of all the city's neighborhoods, Oakland, home to the University of Pittsburgh and its associated hospitals, Carlow University, Carnegie Mellon University, and the Carnegie Museums.

Two East End neighborhoods, Greenfield and South Oakland, abut the north side of the Monongahela River, and there are several extant steps that offer a glimpse of the routes used by the workers from these

Figure 24. Steps Connecting Greenfield Avenue and Waldeck Street

neighborhoods wending their way down to the Jones and Laughlin steel mill on the river banks.

Perhaps the most spectacular set of steps stretched from Second Avenue to Bohem Street, which used to cross Parkway East connecting a highpoint in the South Oakland neighborhood to the former site of the steel mill. The steps were preserved when the parkway was built, but recently the crossing portion of the steps was demolished. The crossing had been reminiscent of crossings provided for the Appalachian Trail over many interstates along the East Coast.

This was not the only accommodation made for the city steps when the Parkway East was constructed in 1952. At that time, the Jones and Laughlin steel mill was active and the Maurice Street steps were still used by the workers. To provide access to these steps a rather substantial, 12-foot-wide pedestrian tunnel was constructed under the six lanes of the Parkway East and the former Baltimore and Ohio railroad tracks (now the Eliza Furnace Recreational Trail). The tunnel, located on Second Avenue across from the Technology Center, approximately 0.25 mile west of Bates Street, is closed today and leads only to vacant land

Figure 25. Sidewalk steps on Nansen Street in Greenfield

between the Parkway East and Forbes Avenue. Road construction and the demise of the steel mill led to the end of the neighborhood served by these steps and the steps themselves. However, a remnant of the steps still survives on a section of Maurice Street near Fifth Avenue.

Farther up river, along Second Avenue in the Greenfield/Hazelwood area, are the Tullymet and Berwick Street steps. A segment of the Tullymet Street steps is shown in Figure 24. These are a few of the other routes workers took to the mill. Perhaps the most interesting set of sidewalk steps in this area are those on Nansen Street (Figure 25). These are undoubtedly one of the most spectacular sidewalk steps in the city, following a steep incline with many high rises. These 152 steps make the ascent of Nansen Street from Flowers Avenue to Hazelwood Avenue possible.

South Side

The area south of the Monongahela River and east of the Fort Pitt Tunnels (in Pittsburgh, locations and directions almost always reference a bridge, tunnel, or river) is the South Side. Although technically encompassing a number of diverse neighborhoods, the South Side ("Sahside," locally) has come to refer to "the Flats," the neighborhood adjacent to the river, and "the Slopes," the high ground beyond. Now a focus of nightlife in Pittsburgh, the Flats area hosted a different nightlife years ago, as it was the location of steel mills and glass factories. The workers, however, lived for the most part on the Slopes. This region of Pittsburgh is dense with city steps, many of which can be seen from across the river.

The South Side Slopes neighborhood, situated above the South Side Flats, typifies the early immigrant neighborhoods perched above the flat areas occupied by the mills. The houses, typically one room wide, several deep, and several stories high packed together on a hillside with many narrow walkways provide a glimpse of the early mill workers' neighborhood. This region has many narrow winding streets and a fairly dense network of city steps that are still in routine use.

This neighborhood, not surprisingly, has the most sets of city steps in Pittsburgh. A map of the sixty-eight sets of steps is shown in Figure 26. The neighborhood values the steps in this area and its neighborhood association plays a robust advocate role. Their annual event, Step Trek,

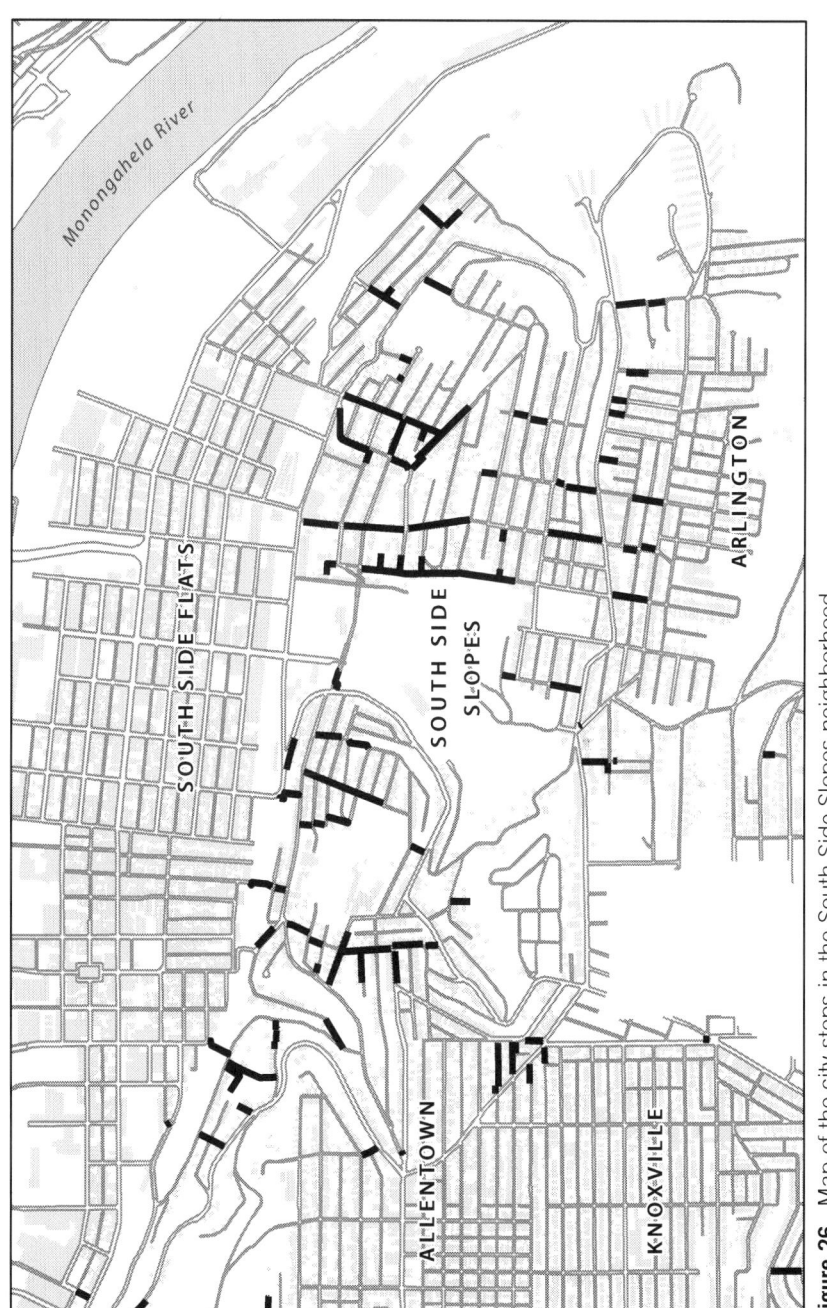

Figure 26. Map of the city steps in the South Side Slopes neighborhood

Figure 27. South 18th Street Steps

draws hundreds of people each year to a casual tour of the steps and neighborhood. The South 18th Street steps (Figure 27) readily announce the entrance to this area and provide a visual clue that steps dominate the neighborhood.

WEST END

The West End is both a formally designated neighborhood and a loose term for that section of the city south of the Ohio River, which has its genesis at "The Point" or the combined terminus of the Allegheny and Monongahela Rivers. Often called the best kept secret in Pittsburgh, this area offers some of the finest views of the city both from bluffs above the river and from the West End Bridge across the river. The West End, like many areas in the southern part of the city, was a region of coal mining activities in the nineteenth century.

An article in the *Pittsburgh Sun Telegraph* (November 20, 1958) talked about steps in this area. "If it is just steps you are looking for, without connecting platforms, it's hard to beat those on Chicken Hill in the

Figure 28. Planet Street

Figure 29. Planet Street

West End. They have 580 feet of steps and extend to Woodville Avenue." Unfortunately, time has not been kind to these steps. Only unusable segments of the steps, the Endness Street steps, remain between Woodville Avenue and Journal Street.

Commuters using Route 60 through the West End have a daily opportunity to view two functional and impressive sets of city steps just off Steuben Street. The Balfour Street steps connect directly to Steuben Street and a walk up these 232 steps accompanied by an additional walk up the 187 steps in the Valonia Street steps near the top brings one close to the West End Overlook with a spectacular view of the city. In approaching the overlook in this fashion, one feels he has earned the view. Nearby is another interesting set of steps, the Planet Street steps shown in Figures 28 and 29.

Historic Sets of City Steps

THE DATES OF CONSTRUCTION ARE KNOWN FOR ONLY 502 SETS OF CITY steps with the oldest dating to 1911. However, the 1884 Sanborn Fire Insurance Maps show twelve sets of city steps in Pittsburgh. The Sanborn Maps Company, headquartered in Pelham, New York, published detailed city maps for fire insurance purposes from 1867 to 1907. The oldest extant Sanborn maps for Pittsburgh are the 1884 maps. Subsequent versions of the Sanborn maps in 1893 and 1905 show a steady increase in the number of city steps.

Without a doubt, the most dramatic set of historic city steps was the Duquesne Heights or Indian Trail steps. These steps, built by the city in 1905 along the side of Mount Washington, extended from Carson Street, near the terminus of the Duquesne Incline, to a point near the intersection of Shaler Street and Grandview Avenue in the Duquesne Heights neighborhood. There were approximately 1,000 steps on this almost mile-long wooden stairway. Unfortunately they were dismantled in 1935, but some remnants still exist along the hillside. The steps were used by mill workers to walk down to work and at the end of the day to walk home up to Grandview Avenue. The workers tended to shun the Duquesne Incline, as it cost 5 cents to ride. As Ernie Pyle noted in his historic 1937 column about Pittsburgh, "The well-to-do people drive to work. The medium people go on streetcars and inclines. . . . And the poor people walk up the steps."

The story, perhaps an urban legend, is that to encourage workers to use the incline, operators of the Duquesne Incline spread a rumor that the steps were along an old haunted Indian trail. They subsequently

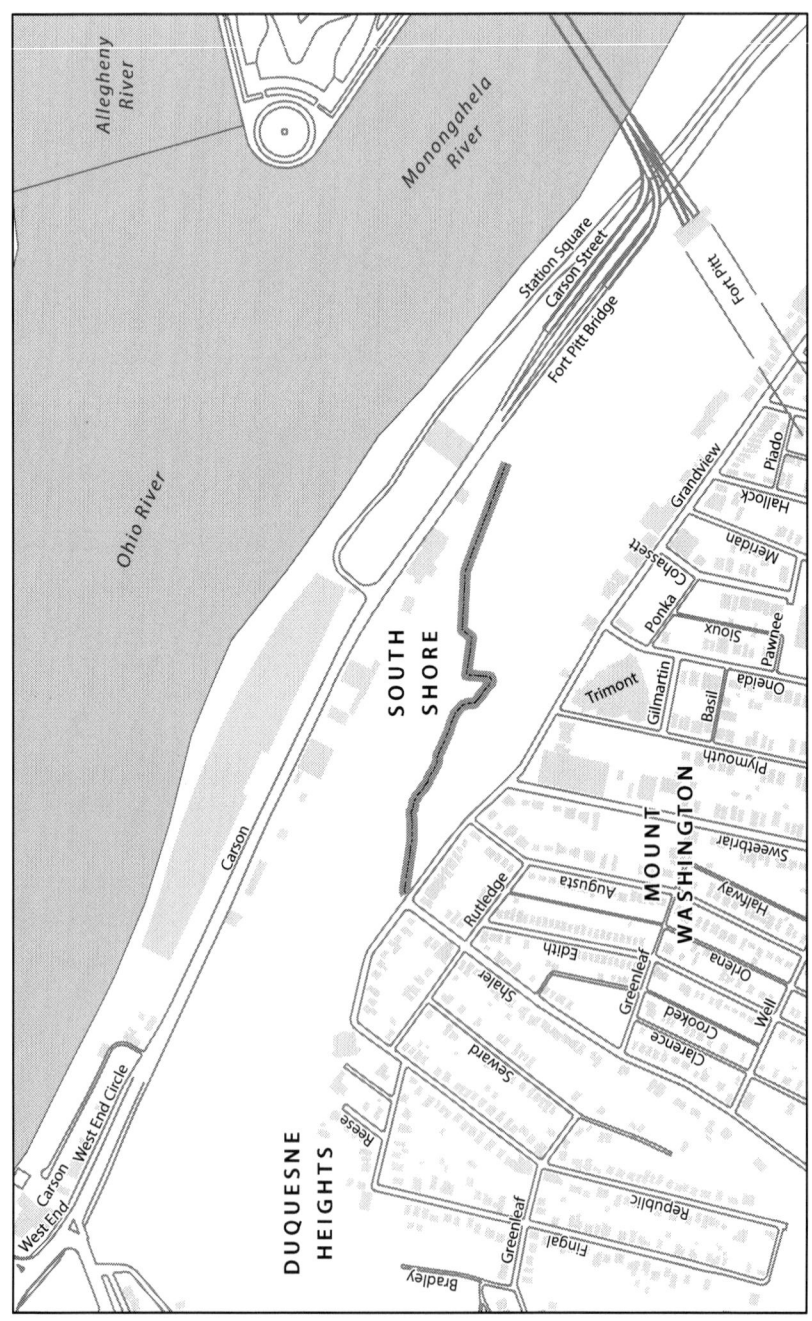

Figure 30. Map Showing location of the Historic Indian Trail Steps

Figure 31. Historic photo of the Indian Trail Steps

became known as the Indian Trail Steps. A map of the location of these steps and a picture of them is shown in Figures 30 and 31.

It must have been a workout to traverse these steps at any time, let alone at the end of a twelve-hour day. Undoubtedly it would have been easier if the mills were on the high ground and the homes on the lowland as then the journey at the end of a day would have been downhill and not up. One can only wonder what those who traveled these and other city steps on a routine daily basis would think if they could see the Pittsburgh citizens today exercising on machines at health clubs.

It is interesting to note that the Sanborn Fire Insurance maps accurately displayed the street steps as steps. However, these maps were never used for driving directions or navigation purposes. The paper road maps, an example of which was shown in Figure 7, all show the street steps as complete streets. Today, the various computer-based maps, such as Google maps, correctly depict the street steps as steps. This is due to the work and input of many steps advocates as well as to the use of more sophisticated mapping technologies.

INCLINES

Prior to 1870 the Mount Washington area of the city was only accessible by city steps or a narrow, muddy path cut into the hillside. However, this changed with the construction of the Monongahela Incline, so named because it ran from the Monongahela Borough (today's Pittsburgh's South Side) to Mount Washington. Built in 1867, three years before San Francisco cable cars, it was the first passenger incline in Pittsburgh and the first in the United States and remains today as the oldest extant municipal incline.

The Mount Washington area, being among the steepest in the city, was a natural choice for the first incline. However, another factor influencing the choice of this locale was that the majority of the immigrant workers in this area were from Germany and thus familiar with inclines, or *steilbahns,* from their native land.

The Duquesne Incline, built in 1877, was the third of Pittsburgh's passenger inclines to be built. Although it was rebuilt in 1888, the cars, which still operate today, are the original cars of the incline. The incline persists today thanks to the Herculean efforts, and ongoing work, of the Society to Preserve the Duquesne Incline.

At one time the city had seventeen notable inclines; additionally there were some smaller ones used to carry coal. Also records show fifteen or more incline companies that were formed but never built the proposed inclines. Pittsburgh inclines were of a great variety, including one with one car, one with no motor, one with no cars (Castle Shannon South), and two with curves. The seventeen historic inclines are shown in Figure 32. It is worthy of note that one historic incline, the Fort Pitt Incline, was replaced in 1919 by a set of city steps. These run along the old incline route from Second Avenue, near the Armstrong Tunnel, up to Bluff and the connecting pedestrian bridge to Duquesne University.

CITY STEPS IN OTHER CITIES

Across the country there seems to be a renaissance of interest in city steps or public stairways. Undoubtedly this is due to the recognition of such assets as an integral part of civic pride and in part to the continuing exercise craze. There are a host of websites, books, and other publications

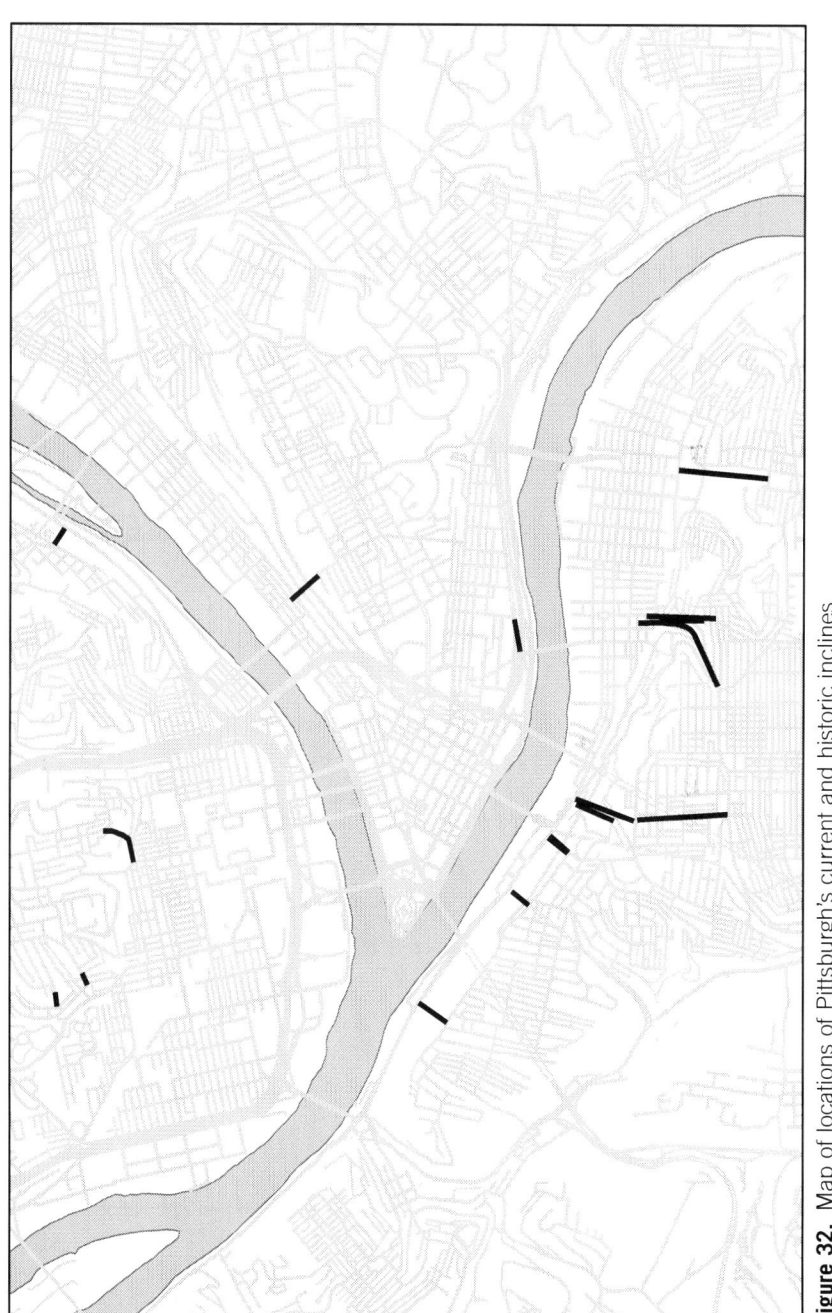

Figure 32. Map of locations of Pittsburgh's current and historic inclines

Figure 33. Steps part of a neighborhood

devoted to this subject. The most prominent, and all inclusive, website is publicstairs.com, a veritable plethora of information. The site's records section lists the number of major stairways, defined as having 100 steps or more, for several US cities. The list shows that Pittsburgh, Pennsylvania, has 117; Los Angeles, California, has 89; Seattle, Washington, has 85; and San Francisco, California, has 79. However our analysis indicates that if sidewalk steps were included, the number for Pittsburgh would be 135 major stairways. Incidentally, the public stairs website offers free "I Take the Stairs" buttons. All one has to do to obtain a button is email a request to beyerlein@comcast.net.

In examining the information on the public stairways in the other cities it was noted that, in many cases, no clear definition of public stairways was included in the information. Consequently the totals may include steps in parks and privately owned stairways that are publicly accessible. With this caveat in mind we present information on the steps in these other cities.

Bob Inman, in his book *A Guide to the Public Stairways of Los Angeles,* reports that the hilly residential areas of Los Angeles contain more than 260 public stairways. Jake and Cathy Jarmillo, in their book *Seattle Stairway Walks*, note that there are over 600 publicly accessible stairways within Seattle's city limits. The website sisterbetty.org states that San Francisco hosts 300 stairways. Cincinnati's website reports that there are nearly 400 sets of city hillside stairways (not including those within parks and recreation properties). Furthermore the City of Cincinnati has developed a City Hillside Step Information System as a means of maintaining an inventory of the steps and to track inspection and repairs.

Steps Supporters and Enthusiasts

THE STEPS HAVE GAINED SIGNIFICANT SUPPORT FROM NEIGHBORHOODS within the city and enthusiastic steps visitors from around the country. Civic events featuring the steps or focusing attention on the city steps have done much to call attention to the steps and aid in their preservation. Certainly that was one of the main goals of the Fineview Citizens Council's Stepathon and has been since 1995. A similar event, the City of Pittsburgh Step Trek, has been conducted by the South Side Slopes Neighborhood Association since 2000.

Fineview's Stepathon, an urban step challenge, is a 5-mile run and hike through one of Pittsburgh's most scenic hilly neighborhoods. The

Figure 34. People enjoying the Step Trek

Figure 35. People enjoying the Step Trek

course traverses more than 1,600 steps, including the 331 steps of Rising Main Way. As a result of its many years of support for the city steps, Fineview received a $10,000 grant from the Sprout Fund to create a detailed inventory of the twenty-seven sets of city steps in the neighborhood. The project also involved detailed mapping, signage, and trail markers as well as an assessment of the state of the steps.

The South Side Slopes Step Trek is not a race, but rather a casual exploration of the many hillside steps in the neighborhood. The Step Trek, which attracts hundreds of steps visitors each year, has two routes, one with about 1,200 steps and one with about 1,800 steps. Figures 34 and 35 show images of trekkers along these routes.

The organizers vary the Step Trek routes on a yearly basis to ensure that the planned routes traverse steps in need of repair to force the city's hand in doing so. So far, this strategy has worked, the city has been responsive and many steps in the neighborhood have been fixed. Unfortunately, however, one segment of Cologne Street was deemed too costly to repair and was ultimately closed.

The steps certainly received some publicity when Argentine Productions filmed *Pittsburgh's Big Picture,* a short IMAX documentary. Peter

Figure 36. IMAX film crew at the Gladstone Street steps

Argentine spent several days scouting step locations and shot many scenes of the steps and on the steps. Figure 36 shows the IMAX crew filming at the Gladstone Street steps in Greenfield. However, in true Hollywood fashion, only one step scene was included in the final picture.

Additionally, Cynthia Cooley, a nationally acclaimed artist known for her vivid paintings of Pittsburgh's hillside neighborhoods and industrial valleys, became intrigued with the city steps. Her many paintings of the steps have been featured in several exhibitions, including an entire exhibit of her Pittsburgh steps paintings at the Bird in Hand gallery in Sewickley, Pennsylvania, in 2006. Some of her steps paintings are available for review on her website, cynthiacooley.com. Her colorful paintings shed a whole new light on the city steps of Pittsburgh.

As noted in the preface, literally hundreds of people from around the world have traveled to Pittsburgh to experience the city steps. The stories of two of these enthusiasts are representative of many of the steps visitors.

Angela Bidlack of the North Hills first discovered the steps in April 2009. She and her husband belong to Venture Outdoors and participated in one of the hikes throughout the South Side Slopes steps. As she says, "We loved learning about life on the slopes as well as an overview of the steps in Pittsburgh. The culture and history were so, were so *Pittsburgh*."

She loved the hike and now she and a group of friends are exploring the South Side Slope steps again and plan to explore steps in other Pittsburgh neighborhoods.

Charlotte Watenpool lives in Florida but vacations in Pittsburgh to walk the city steps. Her goal is to walk all 45,454 of them. So far, she and her cousin, Colleen Kulikowski, who lives in Penn Hills, have walked 200 sets of city steps. Charlotte photographically documents each set of steps she walks and one of her goals is to find sets that have not been documented so far. Her other goal is to utilize her experiences and photos to produce a book on her adventures. As she notes, "You get to see the city of Pittsburgh from angles that nobody will see unless they walk the steps, and it is also good for exercise."

State of Pittsburgh Steps in 2015

Pittsburgh's city steps are no different than the other aging infrastructure throughout the United States. They are aging and in need of upkeep and repair. The upkeep and maintenance of such an asset would present a problem to any municipality in these economic times.

Unfortunately, I have been unsuccessful in reaching city officials for comment on the city steps. However, newspaper reporters have been quite successful and in 2014, articles on the city steps appeared in the *Pittsburgh Post-Gazette*, the *Pittsburgh Tribune-Review*, and the *Wall*

Figure 37. Reconditioned Blanton Street steps

Figure 38. New street sign on Saint Michael Street steps

Street Journal. From these, all of which contained interviews with Guy Costa, city operations chief, the following is apparent.

Since 2006, the city has budgeted $200,000 annually for repair of city-owned steps, walls, and fences. The cost of steps repair is high due to the fact that they are not easily accessible for construction equipment; all supplies, including concrete, must be carried up, or down, the steps. Nearly half of the 2014 budget, $98,000, was allocated for repairing the Blanton Street steps in the Greenfield neighborhood (Figure 37) and Round Top Street steps in Crafton Heights. Much to the delight of the Greenfield neighborhood, the Blanton Street steps have been repaired and are once again in daily use.

One encouraging note is that the city hired two interns for the summer of 2014 to accurately survey and assess the state of the steps throughout the city. City employees now continue their work using interactive tablet computers. One discouraging note is that in 2013, under the previous city administration, a section of the Monastery Street sidewalk steps were demolished and replaced with a sidewalk with a grade of 17.5 percent.

Figure 39. Close-up of Saint Michael Street sign

The uproar over this construction, or destruction, project was widespread. It is doubtful that any similar projects will occur again.

The City of Pittsburgh's Department of City Planning has designed new street signs for the city's street steps. The signs were designed to indicate that the street is a set of steps and conversely that the set of steps is a street. The new street sign at the Saint Michael Street steps is shown in Figures 38 and 39.

In addition to the city's efforts, neighborhoods and people are getting involved in steps maintenance and preservation. A good example is the 2012 project of the South Side Slopes Neighborhood Association. The neighborhood's most prominent set of steps rising above South 18th Street was the target of their efforts. The association in concert with the South Side Local Development Corporation developed a plan to light the steps and use them as an inviting gateway to the community. The project, costing $120,000, was funded by the Duquesne Light Company. Now these steps are truly an inviting entrance to the neighborhood, as each stair tread is illuminated by linear LEDs and projectors carpet the stairs in ambient lighting. In June 2014 the association received a

$100,000 grant from Allegheny County's Community Infrastructure and Tourism Fund. The grant, in response to a proposal, was to evaluate the condition of the neighborhood's sixty-eight sets of city steps and to fund necessary repairs.

Furthering Interest in
Pittsburgh's City Steps

OVER THE PAST DECADE MANY IDEAS FOR DRAWING ATTENTION TO THE city steps have been generated by myself and others. Some of these concepts are set forth in this section.

A Pittsburgh tradition is Light Up Night, an annual event marking the beginning of the holiday season. There are still remnants of the Indian Trail steps along the Mount Washington hillside. A wonderful addition to Light Up Night would be to have lights strung along the route of these steps. The spectacle would be visible to all, enhance Light Up Night, and remind Pittsburghers of their heritage.

One dramatic suggestion for drawing attention to the steps was put forth by Jared Friedman, a 2010 graduate of Carnegie Mellon's Architecture program. Jared was one of the two winners of the Pittsburgh chapter of the American Institute of Architects' Young Studio Competition to design a hypothetical set of steps in Pittsburgh. His proposal, entitled *Uncover Pittsburgh,* focused on revitalizing existing steps of the city. In his proposal he wrote, "When people think of Pittsburgh's infrastructure, bridges are likely the first thing to come to mind. Bridges are large, highly visible, and in Pittsburgh they're often a bright yellow. Where there are rivers there are bridges. And where there are hills there are steps . . . 44,645 of them to be exact. While new modes of transportation have lessened the need for many of the steps, there is still much value in restoring them—even if for only recreational purposes. This project proposes a way to transform the existing city steps into iconic landmarks that scatter the city."

Figure 40. *Uncover Pittsburgh*

Figure 41. Steps bumper stickers

Uncover Pittsburgh proposes a large, modular tensile structure that could be placed over any set of city steps. The project targets sets of steps that are in densely vegetated areas, which may be hard to see at first glance. "The peaks of the structure would rise above the trees in order to increase visibility of the stairs, while the base works to block overgrowth onto the steps. In addition to the utilitarian benefits of the structure, the act of trekking the steps would become a memorable and powerful experience likely to cause a buzz." A figure from Jared's proposal illustrating his concept is shown in Figure 40.

As previously noted, in October of each year the South Side Slopes Neighborhood Association holds an annual Step Trek and the Fineview Citizens Council has its annual Stepathon. Both events are designed to highlight and support the city steps. It would be welcoming to see both of these events held on the same weekend and have the city endorse a formal Celebration of City Steps Weekend. Hopefully, other neighborhoods could also join with their own city steps celebrations.

In September 2014 the South Side Slopes Neighborhood Association held a mini Step Trek for the attendees at the Project for Public Spaces' "Pro Walk Pro Bike Pro Place" convention held in Pittsburgh.

In an attempt to publicize the city steps over the past few years, I have produced and distributed several bumper stickers. These are shown in Figure 41. In addition, I think it is important to introduce future generations to this invaluable asset of the city. Toward that end I have prepared a children's book entitled *How the Sad Steps Helped Save Our Steps*. The text of that book in adult form is contained in Appendix B.

The bottom of the unnamed set of steps on Troy Hill that end at Troy Hill Road and Goettman Street is now readily accessible on the new East Ohio Street Walkway. The walkway is adorned with informative historic signs, but there is no sign at the base of these steps, which are among the finest and best preserved in the city. It would serve the city well to place an informative sign about the city steps at this locale.

These are just some of the ideas for drawing attention to the city steps that have surfaced over the past few years. If you have an idea for this, please write a letter to the editor of either the *Pittsburgh Post-Gazette* or *Pittsburgh Tribune-Review*. Both these local newspapers have been strong and vocal supporters of the city steps.

Select Walking Tours

As city steps are best appreciated by a walking tour of some of these colorful neighborhoods, we offer some selected tours of the steps in several neighborhoods.

Fineview

A map of the steps in this neighborhood is shown in Figure 42. A great place to start is at the end of Howard Street, which is adjacent to I-279 and runs off North Avenue. At the end of Howard Street near the city's public works building is the intersection with Rising Main Way. The Rising Main Way steps (shown in Figure 20) start as sidewalk steps but soon become street steps. Climbing these 331 steps, equivalent to climbing 17 floors in a building, brings you to Warren Street. The Rising Main steps continue across Warren Street but as 31 wooden sidewalk steps.

Continue up to Lanark Street, turn right, and go to Marsonia Street and turn left. There are unusual high sidewalk steps at the intersection of Marsonia Street and Osgood Street (41 steps on Marsonia Street and 27 steps on Osgood Street). These steps are worth exploring.

Travel back to Lanark Street, turn right, and continue down Lanark Street. At the end of Lanark Street is a set of 19 sidewalk steps. At their end, turn left onto Catoma Street and then left on Warren Street.

Turn right onto Carrie Street and walk to the bend in the road (actually the intersection with Henderson Street). Here is the top of the Carrie Street steps. Explore these 106 steps that were built in 1948, then return to the top and continue down Henderson Street.

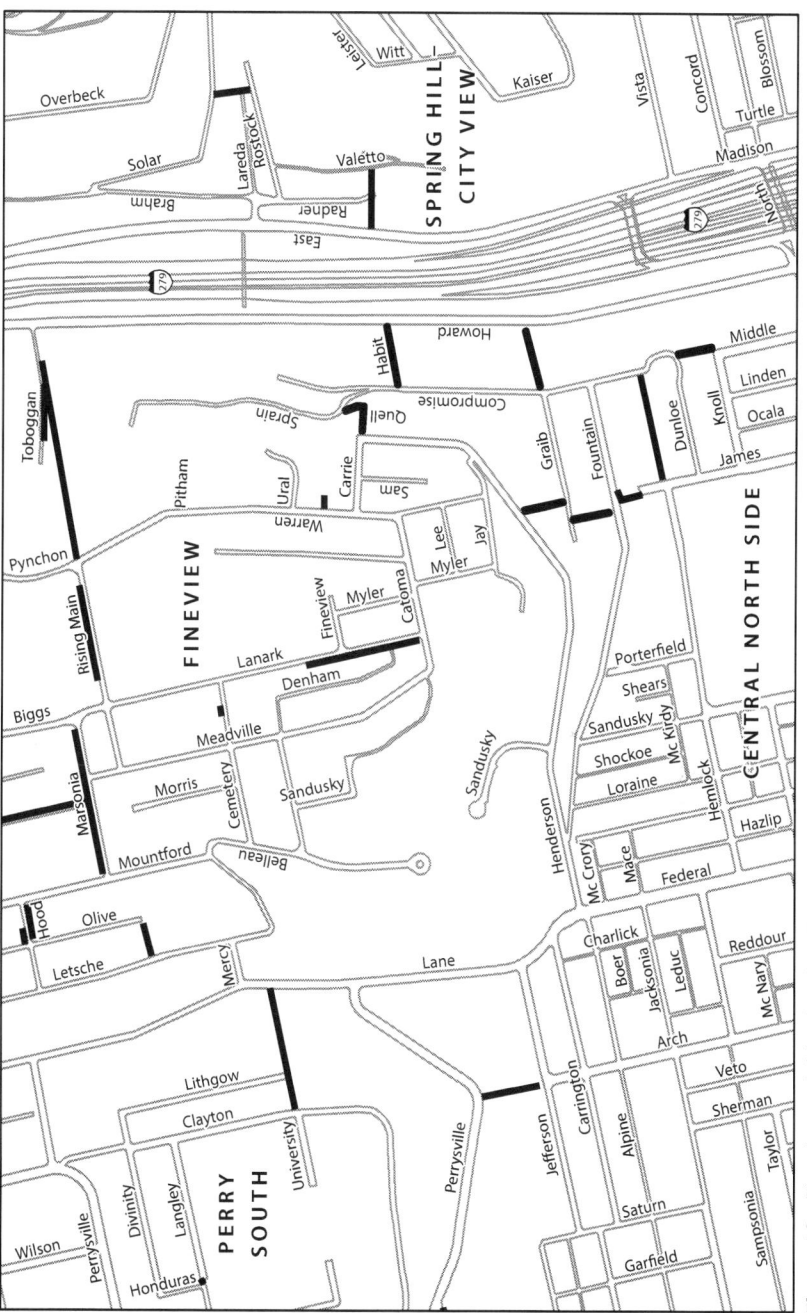

Figure 42. Fineview neighborhood walking tour

After the street turns, look for steps on the left. These 56 steps go down to Graib Street. Turn right and another set of similar steps (51) leads down to Fountain Street.

Turn left at the bottom and travel to the top of the James Street steps. Descend these 62 steps to the "real" James Street. Travel down James Street until you reach the Hemlock Street steps. These steps are unusual, as they go up the hill, reach a peak, and then travel down the other side. Traversing these 143 steps will lead to Compromise Street.

A short distance after turning right on Compromise Street you reach the top of the 101 steps on Middle Street, shown in the cover painting. It is worth the short diversion to witness an unusual view of the city from their top. However, the walking route is in the other direction. Traveling back along Compromise Street there are two sets of steps on the right, Graib Street (146 steps) and Habit Street (144 steps). Either set of these city steps leads back to Howard Street and the beginning of the walking tour.

GREENFIELD

The steps in the Greenfield neighborhood (Figure 43) require more of an exploration than a simple walking tour. The first place to visit is where Greenfield Avenue meets the Swinburne Bridge. The 128 highly visible steps across from the Swinburne Bridge lead up to Downing Street. Traveling up and down these steps provides a workout and offers some good views. A little farther up Greenfield Avenue are the Tunstall Street sidewalk steps. These 28 steps lead up to Alvin Street where 66 steps take you to Yoder Street where you can walk up an additional 128 sidewalk steps. At the top of the Greenfield Avenue hill behind several neighborhood speakeasies are the Coleman Street (128) and Hoosac Street (45) sidewalk steps, which will lead you to wonder how people can park their cars. Further up Greenfield Avenue, across from Magee Field, are the Blanton Street steps. These 107 steps were recently refurbished by the city and are perhaps in the best condition of all the city steps. On the other side of Greenfield are the Gladstone Street steps, an area filmed by the IMAX film crew. These 140 steps are perhaps one of the most scenic sets of steps in the city.

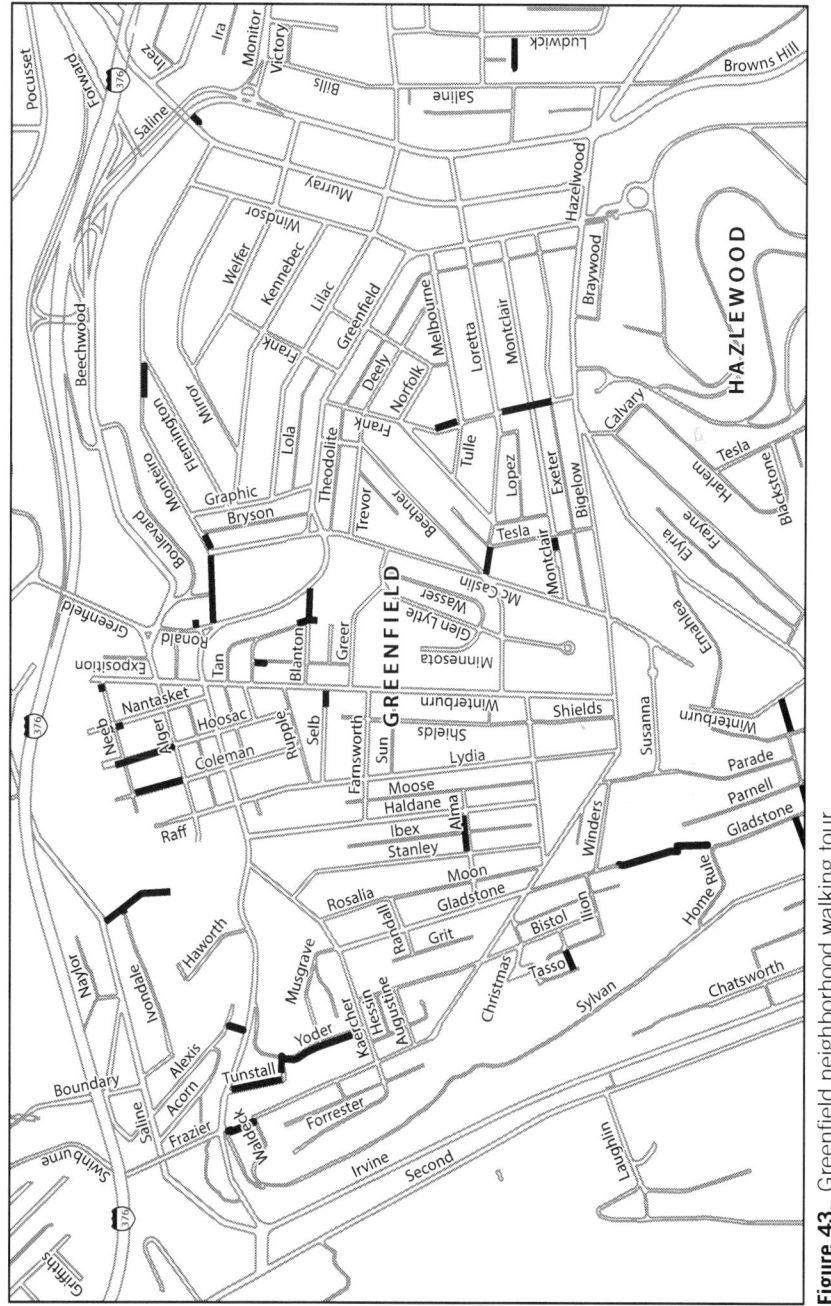

Figure 43. Greenfield neighborhood walking tour

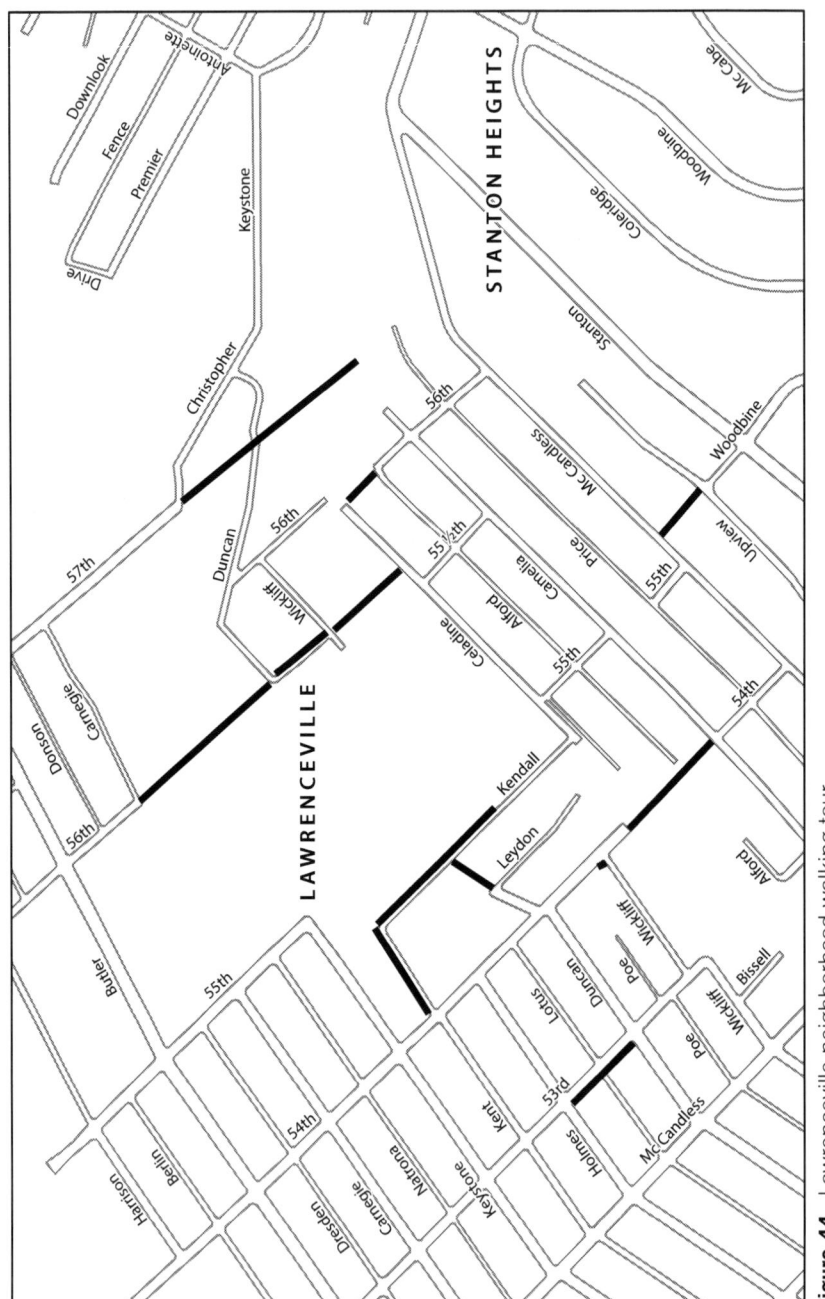

Figure 44. Lawrenceville neighborhood walking tour

LAWRENCEVILLE

This walking tour is shown in Figure 44. A great place to start to explore the steps in Lawrenceville is the Shop 'n' Save market off Butler Street and 56th Street. Fifty-Sixth Street turns into street steps at the intersection with Carnegie Street at the edge of the parking lot. In 2014 these steps were closed for repair (Figure 45). Experience the climb many long-time residents take home from the grocery store as you ascend these 249 steps to Duncan Street. They continue on as sidewalk steps, but before you continue, take a little detour to the left. Walk along Duncan Street, past another 56th Street (true!), to the 57th Street steps. Explore these interesting steps (345 in number) that are complete with houses and mailboxes.

Return to the 56th Street steps and walk up the 26 sidewalk steps to Wickliff Street. Here the steps become street steps again (119) up to Celadine Street. Turn right on Celadine Street to 55 1/2 Street. Turn left to Camelia Street, then turn right and travel down 2 blocks to the 54th Street steps. There are 188 steps down to the "real" 54th Street.

As you continue down 54th Street, notice a little set of 9 steps at the intersection of 54th Street and Wickliff Street. Continue down 54th

Figure 45. 56th Street steps

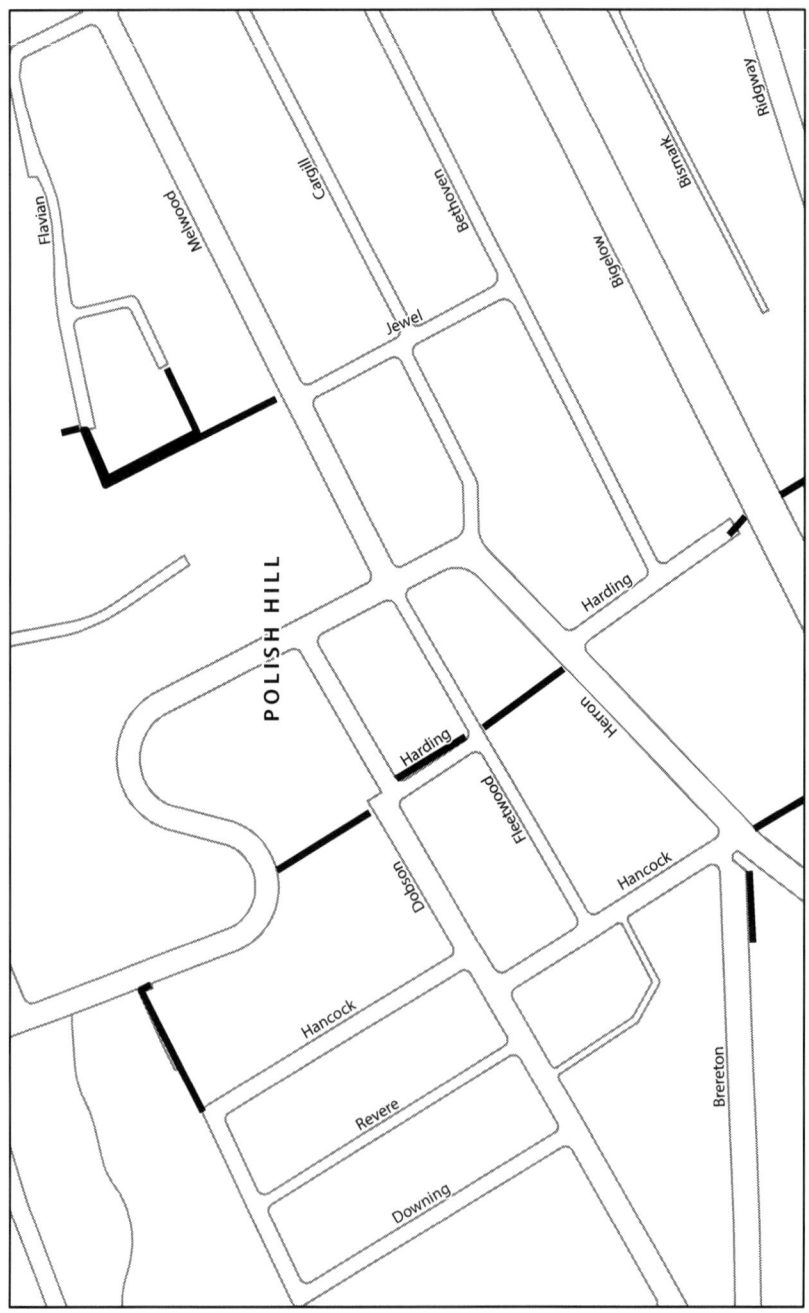

Figure 46. Polish Hill walking tour

Street to Duncan Street. Turn right and walk to the 43 wooden steps that are now Duncan Street and lead to Kendall Street.

Turn right up Kendall Street and walk to the beginning of the spectacular sidewalk steps on the other side of the street. Walk down these 163 steps to the sidewalk steps on Kent Street. These 54 steps bring you back to 54th Street. Turn right and walk down to Carnegie Street. Turn right and find your way back to the Shop 'n' Save market.

POLISH HILL

This is a smaller but interesting walking tour through the intriguing Polish Hill neighborhood. A map of the area is shown in Figure 46. A good place to start is on Herron Avenue near the busway. Undoubtedly one of the most used sets of stairs in the city is the Downing Street steps. Many residents descend the Downing Street steps to Herron Avenue and eventually the busway to commute to work. It is a good trek to take these 81 steps up and then down back to Herron Avenue. A short way up Herron Avenue is the Harding Way steps. Walk up these 80 steps to Dobson Street and then continue up 53 sidewalk steps to Fleetwood. At this point, Hardin Way once again becomes a flight of steps. These 54 steps take you up to Herron Avenue. Turn left and walk down Herron Avenue to Melwood Street. A short walk down Melwood Street and you encounter the 163 Jewel Street steps on the right. Explore the steps and return to Melwood Street. Walk back to Herron Avenue and down to the starting point.

SOUTH OAKLAND

Oakland is at the heart of the East End and offers a chance for many people to sample the steps, which are shown in Figure 47. If you find yourself in the vicinity of the Carnegie Library, walk behind the Frick Fine Arts building (off Shenley Drive) where you will encounter another one of the most used set of steps in the city. These 136 steps provide a daily commuting route for many University of Pittsburgh students who park in the lower part of Oakland (Panther Hollow). The steps, built in 1949, descend to Joncaire Street. At the bottom turn left and then right onto Boundary Street. Walk along Boundary Street. Soon it will turn left

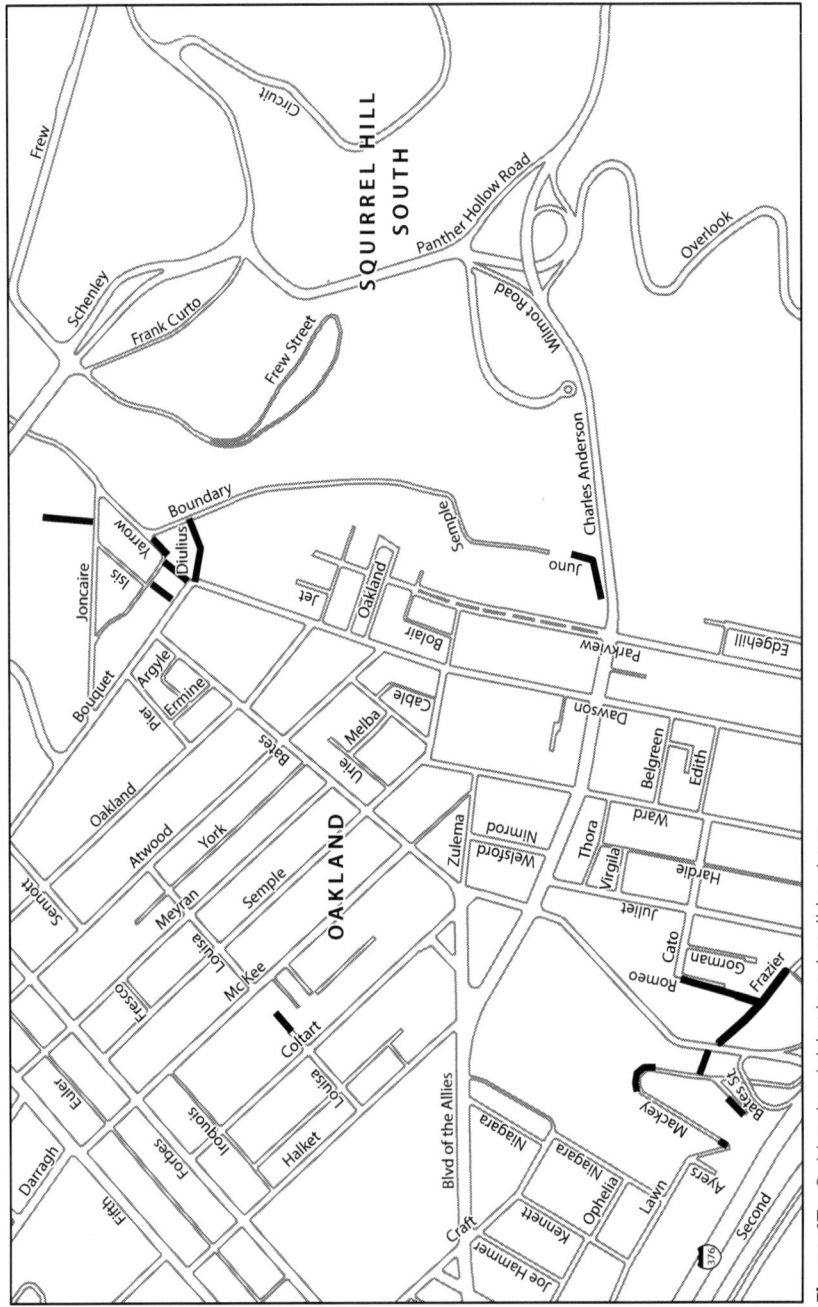

Figure 47. Oakland neighborhood walking tour

and you will notice Diulius Way on the right. These street steps, starting between two houses, are composed of 99 steps leading up to Bouquet Street. Enjoy the labyrinthine feel to the neighborhood houses along this street of steps. Turn right at the top and walk along Bouquet Street until it intersects with Joncaire Street. Turn right and go down Joncaire Street until the first right, which is Yarrow Way. Walk down to the end of Yarrow Way where you will encounter 19 sidewalk steps. These end at Boundary Street, which you can follow back to Joncaire and the 136-step climb back up to the Frick Fine Arts building.

It is worth a short drive to Bates Street near its intersection with Second Avenue to visit the Frazier Street steps. These start (or end depending on your direction of travel) at a bus stop across from the off ramp from the parkway east. It was noticed throughout the step survey that many steps are associated with bus stops. Actually, this was ultimately used as a clue to finding locations of steps.

The Frazier Street steps extend from this point up 117 steps to the end of the conventional Frazier Street. Their intersection, complete with street sign, with the Romeo Street steps makes this an interesting site. The 94 Romeo Street steps extend from Frazier Street (steps) to Cato Street.

SOUTH SIDE

There are many possibilities for walks to explore the steps in the South Side Slopes area. Perhaps the best are the two routes used in the first City of Pittsburgh Step Trek in 2000. These are quite accessible, as there is parking at the beginning of each route. The two routes were labeled the Black Route and the Gold Route. The Black Route (Figure 48) is 2 miles long and encompasses 1,440 steps. You can park near the intersection of 21st Street and Josephine, then walk east on Josephine Street to Greeley Street and turn right. The first steps are partway down Greeley Street on your left. This flight of steps, built in 1947, contains 93 steps that are 4 feet wide. They start at Greeley Street and end at Leticoe Street. At the top of the steps, go straight up Sterling Street to Mission Street.

The first steps on Sterling Street are sidewalk steps. These sidewalk steps extend from Mission Street to Wellington Street and were constructed in 1951. They are also 4 feet wide, and consist of 202 steps. At

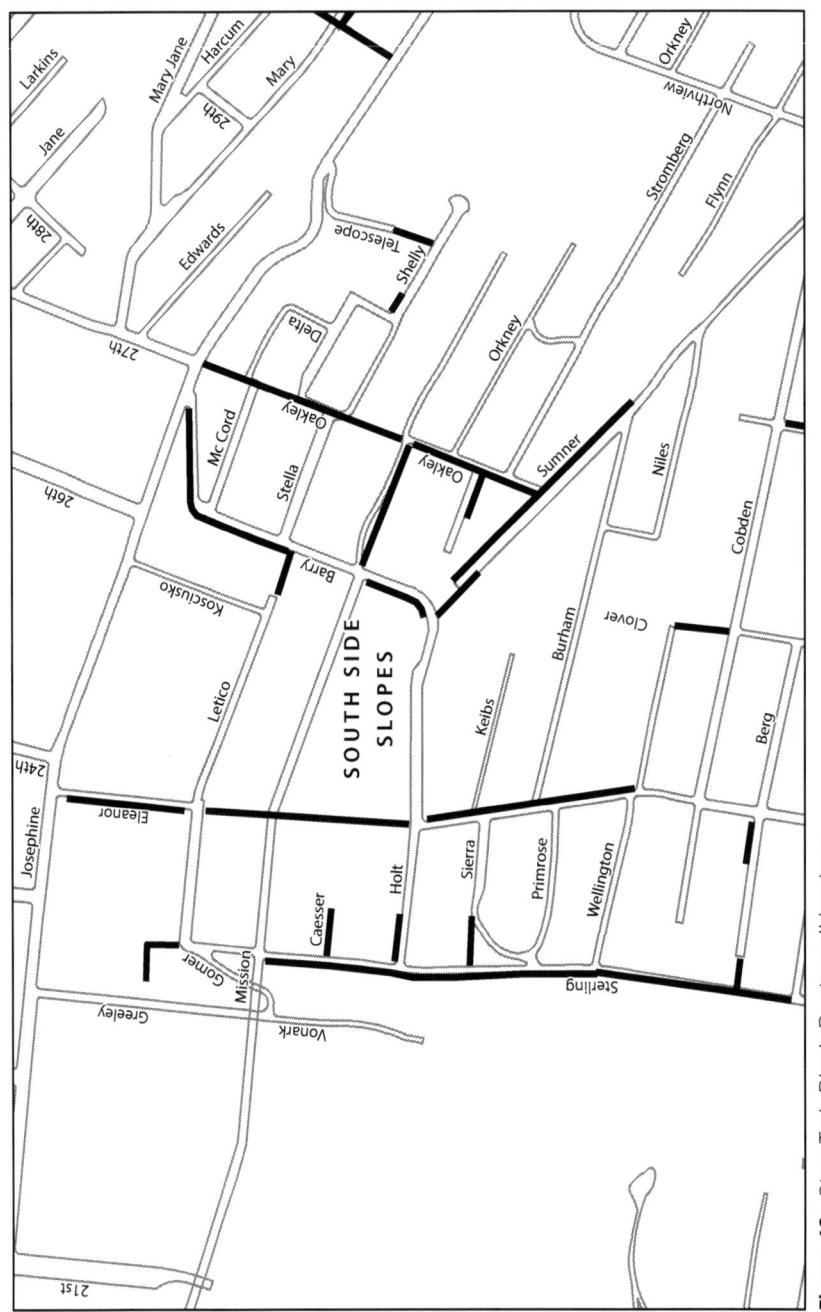

Figure 48. Step Trek Black Route walking tour

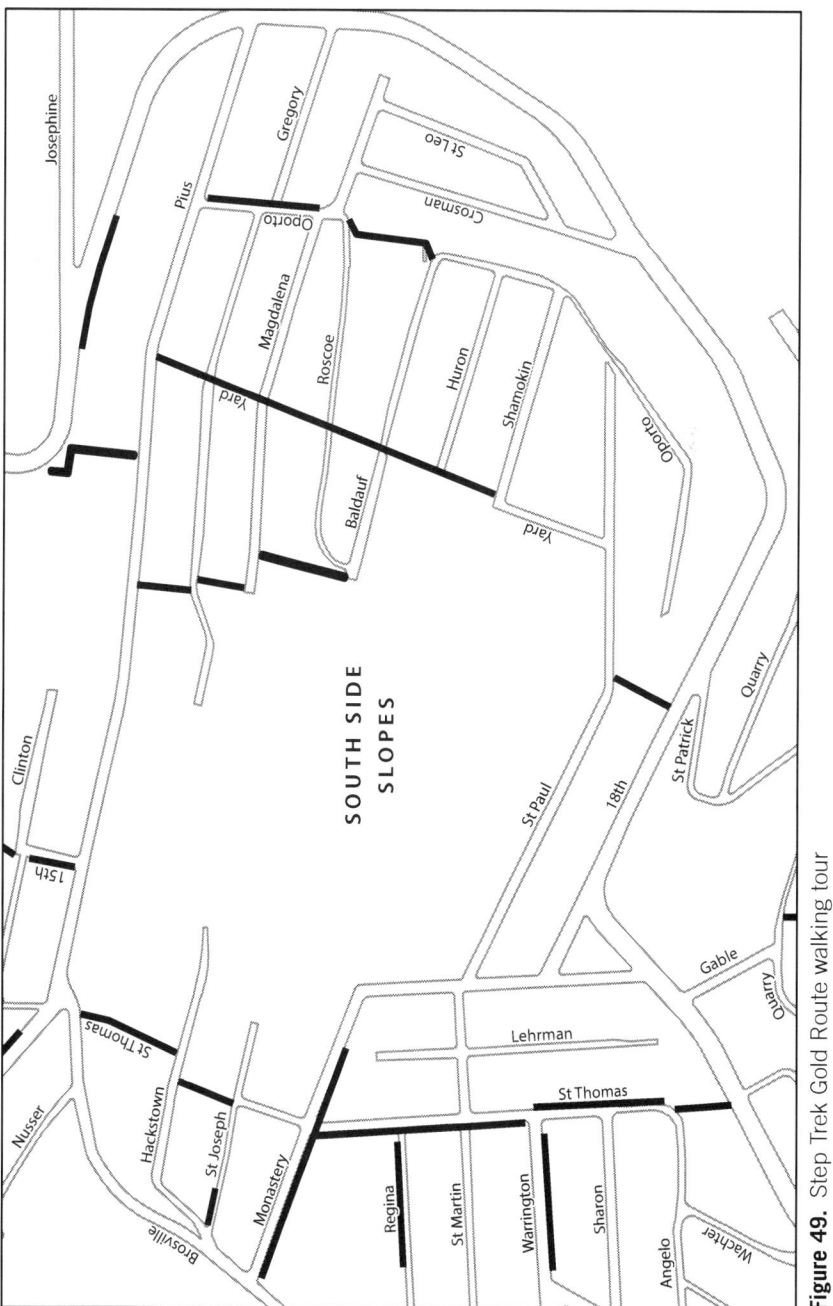

Figure 49. Step Trek Gold Route walking tour

Wellington Street, the Sterling Street steps change from sidewalk steps to street steps and constitute a legal street. These street steps were built in 1951 and extend to Patterson Street. Although the total number of steps is 99, the route traverses only 53 of these steps to the intersection with Berg Street.

The route turns left onto the wooden steps, which are Berg Street. These relatively new street steps were built in 1997 and they number 40. Continue walking along the paved portion of Berg Street and walk the 9 sidewalk steps on the left side down to Eleanor Street. Turn left at Eleanor Street and continue to Codben Street, where the route continues down the sidewalk steps on the right side of Eleanor Street. These sidewalk steps contain the fewest number of steps—exactly one—of any in the city. Although due to the steep slope of the street you will notice a sometimes-much-needed handrail.

Turn right on Holt Street and walk on the sidewalk on the left. Although technically not sidewalk steps, there are 3 steps along this walkway. Cross Holt Street to the flight of steps on the right. These 87 steps, built in 1947, are Sumner Street. At the top of the flight of steps, the Sumner Street steps divide into left and right sidewalk steps. The route traverses the left-hand sidewalk steps. Although these continue all the way to Niles Street, the route turns left onto Oakley Way.

Walk down the 48 sidewalk steps to Mission Street. You might notice the wooden sidewalk steps on Stromberg Street as you pass. Turn left at Mission Street and take the 86 sidewalk steps down to Barry Street. These 4-foot-wide steps were built in 1950 and afford one of the most scenic views on the route. Although the route turns right at Barry Street, notice the sidewalk steps on both sides of Barry Street to the left. Turning right, the route traverses 75 sidewalk steps on the left side of Barry Street. These were built in 1947 and are 5 feet wide.

At the bottom of Barry Street walk east along Josephine Street for a short distance until you encounter the Oakley Way steps on the right. These 285 street steps, built in 1928, reach to Mission Street. However, the route traverses only 248 of these steps (equivalent to 12 floors) to Stella Street. The route turns right along Stella Street and crosses Barry Street to the Leticoe Street steps. These 44 3-foot-wide wooden street steps were built in 1990. At the bottom of the steps, continue west along Leticoe Street until you reach the Eleanor Street steps.

These street steps were built in 1934, number 284, and reach to Holt Street. At the top of the steps the route turns right on Holt Street and traverses 5 cement sidewalk steps to the wooden steps. The Holt Street wooden sidewalk steps are very recent, built in 1999. These 47 steps connect down to Sterling Street where the route crosses to the mid-point of the Sterling Street sidewalk steps.

There are 65 sidewalk steps on Sterling Street from this point to the end of the steps at Mission Street. The last set of steps is the first set of steps and they end at Greeley Street. The route turns right at the bottom and continues to Josephine where it turns left, back to the starting point.

Should you complete this entire route, you will have traversed a 780-foot elevation change, traveled up 950 steps (515 feet) and down 490 steps (265 feet). This is equivalent to having climbed 43 and walked down 22 stories in a building.

The Gold Route (Figure 49) is 2 miles long and contains 1,390 steps. On this route you will walk up 680 steps (370 feet) and down 710 steps (380 feet), which is approximately equivalent to walking up and down 31 stories. Think of traversing the floors of the University of Pittsburgh's Cathedral of Learning as you walk.

Once again you can park near the intersection of 21st Street and Josephine, but then walk west on Josephine Street to South 18th Street and cross. The first steps are the picturesque high flight of steps across the street. This flight of steps was constructed in 1940 and connects South 18th Street to Pius Street. There are 122 steps.

At the top, turn right at Pius Street and walk to South 15th Street. Turn right and take the 11 sidewalk steps on the right side of the street down to Clinton Street. At this point there is the start of the new footbridges (street steps) connecting South 15th Street in the Slopes with South 15th Street in the Flats. This bridge is also South 15th Street (an unusual paper street). Go down these 120 street steps onto the "real" South 15th Street and then turn left on Breed Street. Continue to South 12th Street, where you turn left and start up Brosville Road. Across the railroad bridge there are 42 sidewalk steps on Brosville

Road, which bring you to the intersection of Brosville Road and Pius Street.

Cross the intersection to the Saint Thomas Street steps. There are 115 steps leading up to Saint Michael Street. Continue across Saint Michael Street and take the next set of Saint Thomas Street steps to Saint Joseph Way. This set consists of 78 steps. At this point Saint Thomas Street becomes a "real" street with sidewalk steps. Continue along Saint Thomas Street to Monastery, taking the 6 sidewalk steps on the right.

Cross Monastery Street and take the sidewalk steps on the right. These 65 steps lead almost to Saint Theresa Street. At the end of the steps, cross to the other side of Saint Thomas Street and take the 79 sidewalk steps on this side back to Monastery. These steps afford one of the most scenic views of the walk (indeed of almost any place in the area).

Turn right at Monastery and take the sidewalk steps on the right side. These number 32 and were built in 1950. At the top of the steps continue along Monastery Street past Saint Paul Street to South 18th Street, where the route turns left. Walk down South 18th Street to a set of steps on the left. These steps, built in 1970, connect South 18th Street to Saint Paul Street.

There are 76 steps up to Saint Paul Street. Turn right on Saint Paul Street and walk to Yard Way. Turn left on Yard Way and walk to Shamokin Street. The Yard Way street steps, built in 1944, contain a total of 317 steps and extend from this intersection down to Pius Street. The route continues down 115 of these steps to Baldauf Street.

At Baldauf Street turn left and cross through the playground to Short Street. These street steps were constructed in 1990 and bring you 105 steps down to Magdalena Street. Turn right at the bottom of the steps and walk on Magdalena Street back to Yard Way.

Turn right at the Yard Way steps and walk up the 148 steps to Baldauf Street. At Baldauf Street turn left and walk to the Oporto Street steps. These 124 steps date to 1950 and lead down to Roscoe Street. At the bottom, turn right and cross down to Magdalena Street. Turn left onto Magdalena Street and walk back to the Yard Way steps.

Turn right onto the last segment of the Yard Way steps. These 54 steps connect Magdalena Street to Pius Street. Turn right on Pius Street and walk to South 18th Street. The last set of steps connects the intersection of South 18th Street and Mission Street to South 21st Street. Walk down these 102 steps (built in 1950) and continue onto South 21st Street. A left turn leads back to the start of the route.

SPRING GARDEN

The steps in the Spring Garden neighborhood (Figure 50) offer a true adventure. Start at the intersection of Spring Garden Road and Arcola Way. Walk up Arcola Way to the 15 sidewalk steps and then up the 192 steps of Arcola Way. At the top, turn right onto Diana Street and walk to the end of the paved road. Continue down the spectacular Diana Street steps, all 108 of them. At the bottom, turn left and walk up Homer Street to the Steine Street steps. These 105 concrete steps have been replaced (or joined) by the same number of wooden steps. Walk up the regular Steine Street and turn onto Hunnell Street. Continue walking down to the 50 Hunnell Street sidewalk steps, then walk down the 66 Hunnell Street steps to Yetta Street. Turn right and walk down to the Lappe Lane steps. These 222 steps bring you down to Goerhing Way. Turn left and walk back to the Arcola Way steps and the beginning. In traversing this path you have encountered 970 steps.

WEST END

The steps in the West End are quite impressive, and walking them offers some dramatic views of the area. Park on Main Street near the intersection of Noblestown Road (Route 50 where the Kerr Street steps, soaring steps visible from a large area of the neighborhood, seem to dominate this intersection). A walk up and back down these 199 steps, pausing to enjoy the views along the way, will start your heart pumping and have you anxious for further exploration. From there, walk down Main Street and turn left on Planet Street. The dramatic Planet Street steps several blocks ahead will be quite visible. Traverse up and down these 133 55-year-old steps and enjoy the scenery. Back at the bottom, walk down to Steuben

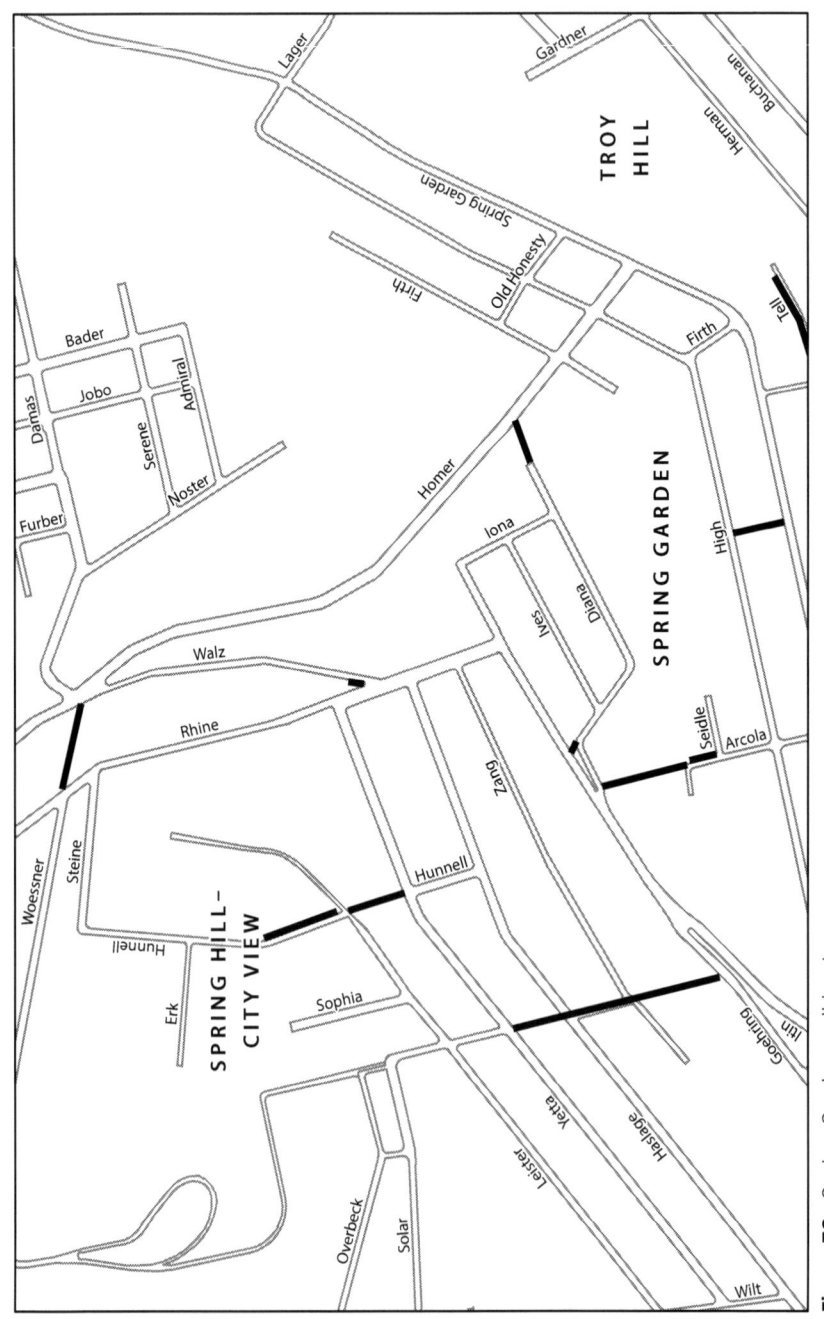

Figure 50. Spring Garden walking tour

Street, turn left, and walk to the bus stop that marks the beginning of the Balfour Street steps.

Walk up these 232 steps and turn right on Landon Street. The next left will bring you to Attica Street and, in a short distance, the base of the Valonia Street steps. Climb these 187 steps and then walk up Valonia Street to Fairview Street. A right turn and a short walk will bring you to the West End Overlook, which offers much more than a fair view of Pittsburgh.

In time, walk back down Fairview Street to the end and descend the 101 Fairview Street steps to Furley Street. Turn left and walk down Furley Street to Attica Street, where a right turn will bring you to the top of a set of 90 steps that lead down to Steuben Street. At the bottom, turn left and just around the corner you will find Planet Street.

Epilogue

The steps are an integral part of the city's history, and should be a source of civic and neighborhood pride. They could, and should, be a major tourist attraction. In today's economic climate many municipalities are striving to identify features and/or events that distinguish their cities for reasons of civic pride and development of tourism. At the same time there are also many movements within municipalities to preserve sources of cultural heritage. Indeed, Robert McNulty, president of Partners for Livable Communities, regularly cites "uniqueness of place" as integral to the success of a city. Pittsburgh is in a position to accomplish these goals by embracing the city steps.

Jake and Cathy Jaramillo, co-authors of *Seattle Stairway Walks*, note that properly maintained stairways are a neighborhood social magnet; they're fun for visitors to explore; they connect residents to parks, stores, and transit; and they provide great outdoor exercise (walking up stairs burns more than three times the calories compared to level walking). Stairways are a distinctive feature of just a handful of American cities. It is terribly short-sighted to let these urban assets deteriorate.

Adah Bakalinsky, author of a guidebook to San Francisco's city steps, spoke with Patricia Lowry of the *Pittsburgh Post-Gazette*, saying that while city steps are her "favorite urban artifact," she only thinks of them in the context of her first love, the neighborhood. Public steps, she explained, are prized because they lead to country-like enclaves, hidden houses, neighborly hill dwellers, and otherwise inaccessible vistas.

San Francisco's steps, not susceptible to damage from severe weather, are built with a wider variety of materials, including wood and stone. But San Francisco's steps don't have the sculptural, zigzagging effect of

Pittsburgh stairways, Bakalinsky said, or steps leading off of steps, as she saw on Rising Main Avenue and Toboggan Street.

What can Pittsburgh do to improve its public steps? First, cut back the overgrowth. A wet spring and summer have resulted in abundant vegetation on Pittsburgh hillsides, some of it spilling over railings and onto steps. Unlike San Francisco, there's so much greenery here. It's a shame that it's overloaded and plants don't get a chance to breathe. Second, Bakalinsky said, she suggests painting the hand railings some color other than the faded blue-green that prevails. The same railing even could be painted several different colors, calling attention to the steps and brightening the hillsides.

However, the real answer to preserving these uniquely historical yet functional features is you. In today's electronic age there are many types of interactive media. Although the printed word is not typically thought to be interactive, perhaps this book can be considered so. If you've read this far you are undoubtedly interested in or intrigued by the city steps of Pittsburgh. So, interact. Walk the steps and feel a linkage with the past, sense the presence of those who daily trod these same structures. At the same time, treat yourself to some of the best scenic views in the area. Tell people about the steps and invite them to explore these features. And, feel a sense of pride that you are in a city that has such features and does what it can to preserve them.

But, perhaps don't settle for that. Interact with the city fathers and the media and call for more. The steps embody the history, romance, intrigue, and energy of Pittsburgh and are a symbol of this great city. However, the city steps are in trouble, as they are not aging well due to the ravages of time and weather. Only you can help.

References

Aurand, Martin. 2014. *The Spectator and the Topographic City*. Pittsburgh, Pennyslvania: University of Pittsburgh Press.

Jaramillo, Jake and Cathy Jaramillo. 2012. *Seattle Stairway Walks*. Seattle, Washington: Mountaineers Books.

Inman, Bob. 2010. *A Guide to the Public Stairways of Los Angeles, 2nd ed.* Retrieved from Blurb.com.

Regan, Bob. 2004. *The Steps of Pittsburgh*. Pittsburgh, Pennsylvania: The Local History Company.

Complete Inventory of Pittsburgh's City Steps

This inventory is from surveys conducted by the author. In June 2015, the City of Pittsburgh began a program, using city employees and volunteers, to do a comprehensive survey of the city steps.

STREET NAME	FROM STREET	TO STREET	STEPS	YEAR
Inglenook Place	Bricelyn Street	Calistoga Street	273	1950
Nimick Place	Oakwood Street	Sickles Street	201	1944
	Singer Place	Sickles Street	124	1949
North Lang Avenue	Haverhill Street	Singer Street	109	1949
	Oakwood Street	Haverhill Street	31	1949
Sterret Street	Chaucer Street	Apple Street	75	1940
North Homewood Avenue	Mount Vernon Street	Upland Street	55	1948
	Upland Street	Saxon Way	43	1948
Monticello Street	Brushton Avenue	Monticello Street	173	1945
	Perchment Street		38	
Lawndale Street	Frankstown Road	Perchment Street	90	1949
Ferndale Street	North Wheeler Street	Willing Street	85	1950
	Lincoln Avenue	Point View Street	142	1946
Toga Way	Lemington Avenue	Westmoreland Avenue	91	1944
Oberlin Street	Lemington Avenue	Somerset Street	50	
LaPorte Street	LaPorte Street	Verona Boulevard	24	
	Beeler Street		60	
	Forbes Avenue	Gladstone Road	90	
	Joncaire Street	Frick Art Museum	136	
Diulius Way	Boundary Street	Bouquet Street	99	1949
Yarrow Street	Yarrow Way	Bouquet Street	45	1949

STREET NAME	FROM STREET	TO STREET	STEPS	YEAR
Yarrow Street	Boundary Street	Yarrow Way	19	1984
Louisa Street	Coltart Avenue	McKee Place	34	1947
Linden Lane	Wilkens Avenue	Linden Lane	42	1947
	Wilkens Avenue	Glen Arden Drive	57	1930
Harding Street	Herron Avenue	Dobson Street	80	1949
	Brereton Street	Paulowna Street	60	1950
Downing Street	Herron Avenue	Hancock Street	81	1948
	Brereton Street	Herron Avenue	7	1940
Apollo Street	Melwood Avenue	Bethoven Street	98	1947
Jewel Street	Flavian Street	Melwood Avenue	163	
			13	
Hancock Street	Herron Avenue	Bigelow Boulevard	50	1952
	Herron Avenue	Bigelow Boulevard	38	1970
	Dobson Street	Fleetwood Way	53	1944
Harding Way	Harding Way	Bigelow Boulevard	27	1949
Harding Way	Bigelow Boulevard	Ridgway Street	71	1944
Croessus Way	East Busway	Flavian Street	54	
30th Street	Paulowna Street	Bigelow Boulevard	85	1948
Finland Street	Bigelow Boulevard	Ridgway Street	109	1945
Orion Way	Monroe Street	Webster Avenue	126	
	Bryn Mar Road	Clarissa Street	69	1949
Alpena Street	Bigelow Boulevard	Andover Terrace	47	1937

STREET NAME	FROM STREET	TO STREET	STEPS	YEAR
30th Street	Bigelow Boulevard	Leander Street	106	1948
Colmar Street	Bernhardt Way	Balboa Street	47	1949
Harry Street	Bernhardt Way	Lisbon Street	41	1950
	Andover Terrace	Dakota Street	18	
Iowa Street	Centre Avenue	Ewart Street	52	1950
	Herron Avenue	Bedford Avenue	13	
Junilla Street	Verdant Way	Webster Avenue	32	1948
Watt Street	Centre Avenue	Elba Street	63	1947
Ewarts Way	Centre Avenue	Breckenridge Street	56	1947
Francis Street	Centennial Way	Webster Avenue	46	1950
	Canton Street	Lilac Street	23	1960
	Lilac Street	Rosemoor Street	32	1960
Murdoch Road	Hobart Street	Guarino Road	10	1950
Steelview Avenue	Brownshill Road	Imogene Road	43	1950
Tell Street	Voskamp Street	Buchanan Street	162	1949
Tell Street	Tell Street	Voskamp Street	26	
Savina Street	Spring Garden Avenue	High Street	51	1949
Harpster Street	Lager Street	Claim Street	45	1949
Lappe Lane	Spring Garden Avenue	High Street	74	1954
	Kennard Field	Waring Court	51	1950
Iowa Street	Centre Avenue	Avalon Street	50	1950
Arcola Way	Seidel Street	Diana Street	192	1950

STREET NAME	FROM STREET	TO STREET	STEPS	YEAR
Diana Street	High Street	Seidel Street	15	1948
	Homer Street	Diana Street	108	1946
Rothlein Way	Spring Garden Avenue	Carrie Street	41	
Basin Street	Welser Way	Voskamp Street	40	1982
Basin Street	Voskamp Street	Brabec Street	188	1950
	Province Street	Goettman Street	93	1950
	Vinial Street	Province Street	177	
Loretto Street	Beechwood Boulevard	Murray Avenue	88	1928
Montclair Street	McCaslin Street	Tesla Street	22	2003
Mohawk Street	Tesla Street	McCaslin Street	8	
Allequippa Street	5th Avenue	Beelen Street	77	1949
	Allequippa Street	Dead End	69	1947
Steine Street	Homer Street	Rhine Street	105	1955
	Robinson Street	Burrows Street	157	
	Second Avenue	Bluff Street	179	1919
	Butler Street	Baker Street	61	1958
	Butler Street	Sawyer Street	87	
	Butler Street	Sawyer Street	87	1948
57th Street	Christopher Street	Camelia Street	345	1949
56th Street	Carnegie Street	Duncan Street	249	1946
	Kent Street	Duncan Street	163	1951
Duncan Street	Leydon Street	Kendall Street	43	1940

STREET NAME	FROM STREET	TO STREET	STEPS	YEAR
54th Street	Wickliff Street	Camelia Street	188	1950
	54th Street	Wickliff Street	9	
Bluebell Street	Perrysville Avenue	Amos Way	61	1940
Montana Street	Grizella Street	Swanson Street	47	1964
Grizella Street	Bonvue Street	Waldorf Street	39	1960
	South Dallas Avenue	Glen Arden Drive	30	1933
	Lincoln Avenue	Washington Boulevard	93	
	Farmhouse Road	Bunker Hill Street	21	
	Heath Street	King Avenue	23	1976
Elgin Street	King Avenue	Elgin Street	22	
	54th Street	Kendall Street	35	
Harding Street	Fleetwood Way	Herron Avenue	53	
	Herron Avenue	Wylie Avenue	12	
	Ossipee Street	Lyon Street	50	
	Centre Avenue	Bryn Mar Road	6	
	Bigelow Boulevard	Schenley Farms Terrace	49	
	University Drive	Allequippa Street	23	
	Morningside Avenue	Duffield Street	33	1949
Adelphia Street	Morningside Avenue	Duffield Street	45	1940
Martha Street	Duffield Street	El Paso Street	105	
Gribble Street	Dewey Avenue	Waldorf Street	160	1946
Lappe Lane	Southside Avenue	Fayban Street	61	

STREET NAME	FROM STREET	TO STREET	STEPS	YEAR
Lappe Lane	Fayban Street	Shirls Street	56	
Girdley Way	Royal Street	Brahm Street	258	1949
Milroy Street	Bothwell Street	Viola Street	92	1982
	Milroy Street	Perrysville Avenue	25	1936
	Heim Street	Bessie Avenue	63	1950
	Baytree Street	East Street	26	1950
	Waldorf Street	Radium Street	89	1950
	Lawn Street	Ophelia Street	15	
	Bigelow Boulevard	Kirkpatrick Street	115	1949
Dressing Way	Marietta Street	Premo Street	90	1950
	Holmes Street	Duncan Street	63	1949
	Upview Terrace	McCandless Avenue	79	1950
	Stanton Avenue	McCandless Avenue	47	1972
	Willing Street	Mohler Street	6	
	Broadcrest Drive		110	
	Missouri Street	Evers Drive	21	
	Olivant Street	Playground	90	
	Lincoln Avenue	Arbor Way	57	1945
Nantasket Street	Nantasket Street	Neeb Street	17	1980
	Alger Street	Neeb Street	45	1950
	Alger Street	Neeb Street	128	2000
B Street	Lamont Street	Morrison Street	70	1948

STREET NAME	FROM STREET	TO STREET	STEPS	YEAR
Hyena Street	Saint Marks Place	B Street	13	1945
Marvista Street	Marvista Street	Success Street	166	1951
Marvista Street	Marvista Street	Winifred Street	209	
	Hyena Street	end	53	
			66	
Artmore Street	Artmore Street	Halsey Place	33	
Halsey Place	Colorado Street	Mennheim Street	43	
	Halsey Place (path)	McCook Street	9	
	Ingram Street	Hodgkiss Street	35	1940
	Ridgecrest Road	Brighton Avenue	9	
Eckert Street	Mullins Street	Hartman Street	32	1940
Dickson Street	Pitler Street	Plough Street	43	1948
	Claifornia Avenue	Pitler Street	23	
	Woodland Avenue	Tumbo Way	80	1940
	Pitler Street		32	
	California Avenue		3	
	Ireland Street		35	
	Ireland Street		10	
Wing Way	Wadlow Street	Shadeland Avenue	108	1948
Oakhill Street	Brighton Road	Frederick Street	125	1944
Malden Street	Oxfield Street	Oakhill Street	65	1940
	Lecky Avenue	Malden Street	117	1960

STREET NAME	FROM STREET	TO STREET	STEPS	YEAR
California Avenue	Eckert Street	Knapp Street	119	1923
	Concord Street	Itin Street	11	1982
	Vinial Street		9	1982
	Tell Street	De Raud Street	63	1952
Rising Way	5th Avenue	De Raud Street	55	1990
Wyandotte Street	Wyandotte Street	Terrace Village #1	109	1949
	Neeb Street		7	
	McCaslin Street	Flemington Street	41	1989
	Greenfield Avenue	Bryson Way	48	1940
	Blanton Street	Blanton Street	107	1931
	Minnesota Street	Minnesota Street	19	
Exposition Way	Winterburn Avenue		6	1990
			14	1980
Monteiro Street	McCaslin Street	Greenfield Avenue	107	
	Ronald Street		5	
	Alvin Street	Kearcher Street	128	1950
Alvin Street	Greenfield Avenue	Alvin Street	66	
	Tunstall Street	Yoder Street	28	
	Greenfield Avenue	Waldeck Street	128	1945
Anthony Street	Alexis Street	Greenfield Avenue	110	1947
	Saline Street	Greenfield School	251	1951
Gladstone Street	Home Rule Street	Winders Street	140	1950

STREET NAME	FROM STREET	TO STREET	STEPS	YEAR
Hilltop Street	Gladstone Street	Parnell Street	27	1950
Hilltop Street	Winterburn Avenue	Georgekay Street	84	1949
Tullymet Street	Chance Street	Gladstone Street	259	1948
Berwick Street	Chatsworth Street	Monogahela Street	54	1947
Berwick Street	Monogahela Street	Sylvan Avenue	64	
Cust Street	Sunnyside Street	Shrub Way	52	1948
Cust Street	Second Avenue	Sunnyside Street	69	
Sunnyside Street	Glenwood Avenue	Sunnyside Street	31	1950
Eddington Street	Kilbourne Street	Kinglake Street	170	1949
Dido Way	Flowers Avenue (ext)	Clarion Street	49	1948
	Haldane Street	Stanley Street	21	1950
	Flowers Avenue	Hazelwood Avenue	152	1947
	South 18th Street	Pius Street	122	1940
Yard Way	Pius Street	Shamokin Street	317	1944
	Pius Street	Roscoe Street	112	1990
Oporto Street	Roscoe Street	Baldauf Street	124	1950
Short Street	Magdalena Street	Baldauf Street	125	1990
	Gregory Street	Magdalena Street	35	1970
	South 18th Street	Saint Paul Street	76	
Welsh Way	Welsh Way	Fritz Street	61	1951
Hartford Street	Fritz Street	Hartford Street	77	1999
Saint Joseph Way	Brosville Road	Saint Joseph Way	77	1980

STREET NAME	FROM STREET	TO STREET	STEPS	YEAR
	Monastery Street	East Warrington Avenue	153	
	Angelo Street	East Warrington Avenue	17	
Saint Thomas Street	South 18th Street	Angelo Street	36	1950
	Hackstown Street	Monastery Street	6	
Saint Thomas Street	Pius Street	Hackstown Street	193	
	Brosville Road	Lehrman Way	157	1950
Hartford Street	Hartford Street		41	
Owl Way	Windom Street	Hartford Street	130	1946
	Windom Street		102	
	Greeley Street	Leticoe Street	93	1947
	Mission Street	Wellington Street	202	1951
Sterling Street	Wellington Street	Patterson Street	99	1951
Berg Street	Sterling Street	Berg Street	43	1997
	Sterling Street	Holt Street	47	1999
Eleanor Street	Leticoe Street	Holt Street	282	1934
	Holt Street	Codben Street	1	
	Mission Street	Sumner Street	48	1931
Oakley Way	Josephine Street	Mission Street	285	1928
Sumner Street	Barry Street	Sumner Street	110	1947
	Mission Street	Holt Street	58	1947
	Josephine Street	Mission Street	78	1947
Leticoe Street	Kosciusco Way	Barry Street	55	1990

STREET NAME	FROM STREET	TO STREET	STEPS	YEAR
	Josephine Street	Northview Street	119	1949
	Salisbury Street	Berg Street	80	1949
	Berg Street	Codben Street	98	
Clover Street	Commanche Way	Arlington Avenue	48	1946
	Salisbury Street	Arlington Avenue	3	
Marengo Street	Salisbury Street	Pine Park	25	1946
	Windom Street	Newton Street	130	1946
Lauer Street	Windom Street	Arlington Avenue	165	
Emerald Way	Arlington Avenue	Excelsior Street	100	1945
Behring Street	Arlington Avenue	Newton Street	41	1990
Brossville Road	Welsh Way	Pius Street	42	1950
	Selby Way	McArdel Roadway	27	
	Saint Thomas Street	Mount Oliver Street	34	1950
	Saint Thomas Street	Regina Street	30	1998
	Gabel Street	Kimbol Street	7	1960
Ivondale Street	Ivondale Street	Anthony Street	33	
Isis Way	Yarrow Way	Bouquet Street	62	
Byron Street	Melwood Avenue	Gold Street	14	1949
	Ellers Street	Allequippa Street	13	1970
Lombard Street	Colwell Street	Diaz Way	25	1930
Wick Street	Colwell Street	Diaz Way	35	1940
Chauncey Street	Centre Avenue	Mahon Street	60	

STREET NAME	FROM STREET	TO STREET	STEPS	YEAR
Morgan Street	Centre Avenue	Elba Street	54	1951
Junilla Street	Centre Avenue	Elba Street	106	1911
Lombard Street	Diaz Way	Lombard Street	28	1968
	Spring Street	Arlington Avenue	66	1948
	Spring Street	Elsie Street	17	1980
	Elsie Street	Charcot Street	74	
	Spring Street	Charcot Street	2	
	Eleanor Street	Berg Street	9	1990
	Sumner Street	Niles Street	79	
	Oakley Way	Stromberg Street	24	
	Barry Street	Oakley Way	86	1950
Sierra Street	Sterling Street	Sierra Street	52	1990
Caesar Way	Sterling Street	Caesar Way	52	1980
	South 18th Street	South 21st Street	102	1950
Telescope Street	Telescope Street	Stella Street	56	1951
	Stella Street	Stella Street	8	
	Josephine Street	Leticoe Street	12	
	South 18th Street	South 18th Street	61	1930
South 30th Street	Harcum Way	Josephine Street	149	1945
	South 30th Street	Mary Street	27	1999
Mary Street	Mary Street	Handler Street	121	1950
	Jane Street	Mary Street	114	1947

STREET NAME	FROM STREET	TO STREET	STEPS	YEAR
	Salisbury Street	Commanche Way	50	
	Gold Street	North Craig Street	28	
	North Craig Street	Bigelow Boulevard	7	
	Andover Terrace	Bryn Mar Road	4	
	Andover Terrace		36	
	5th Avenue	Wilkens Avenue	4	
	Johnston Avenue	Naomi Drive	108	
	Johnston Avenue	Ashton Avenue	80	1989
Nordica Street	Steele Court	Ampere Street	31	
	Kilbourne Street	East Elizabeth Street	42	
	Glenwood Avenue	Steele Court	37	1949
	Flowers Avenue	Nansen Street	12	
Maurice Street	Forbes Avenue	Maurice Street	48	1944
Wakefield Street	10 Wakefield Street		8	1950
Jancey Street	Butler Street	Baker Street	137	1950
Gallatin Street	Baker Street	Witherspoon Street	72	1948
	Morningside Avenue	Duffield Street	2	1960
	Morningside Avenue	Nolo Way	91	1948
	Jancey Street	Morningside Avenue	22	1950
	Morningside Avenue	Stanton Avenue	4	1940
	Hodge Street	Bates Street	32	1960
	Hodge Street	Mackey Street	18	1950
	Hodge Street	end	26	1945

STREET NAME	FROM STREET	TO STREET	STEPS	YEAR
Frazier Street	Bates Street	Gorman Way	117	1947
Romeo Street	Frazier Street	Cato Street	94	1947
	Mackey Street	Lawn Street	28	1940
Wakefield Street	66 Wakefield Street		47	1950
Middle Street	Knoll Street	Dunloe Avenue	101	1948
Chestnut Street	Itin Street	Vista Street	97	1944
Lappe Lane	Goehring Street	Yetta Street	222	1948
Waco Way	East Street	Valette Street	134	1948
Carrie Street	Sprain Street	Carrie Street	106	1948
	Graib Street	Henderson Street	56	1948
Graib Street	Howard Street	Compromise Street	146	1948
Hemlock Street	James Street	Compromise Street	143	1949
James Street	James Street	Fountain Street	62	1948
	Fountain Street	Graib Street	89	1948
Habit Way	Howard Street	Compromise Street	144	1947
Rising Main Way	Toboggan Street	Warren Street	331	1945
	Warren Street	Lanark Street	31	1990
	Rising Main Way	Toboggan Street	78	1946
Biggs Avenue	Glenrose Street	Red Way	53	
	Mountford Avenue	Biggs Street	41	
	Marsonia Street	Lafayette Avenue	27	
Hunnel Street	Yetta Avenue	Leister Street	66	1990

STREET NAME	FROM STREET	TO STREET	STEPS	YEAR
Norwood Avenue	Leister Street	Hunnel Street	50	1990
Hawkins Street	Kennedy Avenue	Marshall Avenue	38	1950
Hawkins Street	Perrysville Avenue	Veteran Street	72	1980
Hawkins Street	Ellis Street	Perrysville Avenue	49	1980
	Shelton Street	Ellis Street	55	1950
Kenwood Avenue	Marshall Avenue	Matson Street	80	1980
Kenwood Avenue	Veteran Street	Sherlock Street	26	1965
	Maple Avenue	Hazelton Street	60	1964
	Perrysville Avenue	Maple Avenue	1	
Irwin Avenue	East McIntyre Avenue	end	17	1980
Irwin Avenue	Wilson Avenue	Perrysville Avenue	106	1948
Rolla Street	Melrose Avenue	Chautauqua Court	177	1946
Overlook Street	Strauss Street	Chester Avenue	229	1946
	Irwin Avenue	Yale Street	232	1949
O'Hern Street	Rolla Street	Geranium Street	72	1945
	Buena Vista Street	Perrysville Avenue	140	1948
Kenton Way	Columbia Place	Buena Vista Street	62	1936
Langley Avenue	Arch Street	Perrysville Avenue	131	1948
Kenn Avenue	Federal Street	Clayton Avenue	38	1949
	Honduras Street	Langley Avenue	15	
	Kenn Avenue	Wilson Avenue	20	
	Hillcrest Street	Columbo Street	122	1949

STREET NAME	FROM STREET	TO STREET	STEPS	YEAR
North Pacific Avenue	Jordan Way	Kincaid Street	23	
	Kincaid Street	Broad Way	27	1950
	Kincaid Street	Brown Way	58	1948
North Evaline Street	Brown Way	Rosetta Street	110	
North Winebiddle Street	Rosetta Street	Hillcrest Street	88	
Rosetta Street	Kincaid Street	Rosetta Street	180	1944
Rosetta Street	North Evaline Street	North Winebiddle Street	98	
Rosetta Street	North Winebiddle Street	North Milvale	146	
North Evaline Street	Rosetta Street	Hillcrest Street	60	1948
Noah Street	Phelan Way	Tasso Street	20	1945
Elora Way	Jordan Way	Kincaid Street	7	1950
	5th Avenue	Warrick Terrace	98	1950
	Ives Way	Itin Street	14	1980
Cedarville Way	Jupiter Street	Lorigan Way	20	1952
Ella Street	Lorigan Way	Minerva Street	97	1949
Wertz Way	Ella Street	Wertz Way	14	1949
Government Way	40th Street	Government Way	9	1948
	Breesport Road	Ft Pitt School	21	1954
	E Ohio Street	Ley Street	167	1950

STREET NAME	FROM STREET	TO STREET	STEPS	YEAR
	Rialto Street	Lowrie Street	20	1949
Purse Way	Harpster Street	Hatteras Street	48	1950
	Herman Street		17	1950
	E Ohio Street	Troy Hill Road	188	
	High Street	Itin Street	4	
	Forbes Avenue		18	
Heckleman Street	E Ohio Street	Eggers Street	?	1950
	Croft Street	Lautner Street	10	1960
	Goettman Street	Truax Way	10	1929
Rankin Avenue	Fleming Avenue	Kalorama Way	71	1949
	Richardson Avenue	Bainton Street	123	1947
Gass Avenue	Woods Run Avenue	Reuben Street	69	1947
Sorento Street	Minott Street	Sorento Street	55	1948
Westborn Street	Palen Way	Grand Avenue	28	
Westborn Street	Central Avenue	Mitchell Street	15	1950
	Smithton Avenue		28	
Westborn Street	Mitchell Street	Rothpeltz Street	39	1948
	Hall Street		71	
	Reuben Street	Beckham Street	44	
Wapello Street	Aquatic Way	Termon Avenue	50	1943
	Termon Avenue		31	
Wapello Street	Termon Avenue	Cornell Street	58	1949

STREET NAME	FROM STREET	TO STREET	STEPS	YEAR
Wapello Street	Benton Avenue	West Pointe Avenue	53	1945
Saint Ives Street	Sedgewick Street	Oriana Street	74	1946
	Morrison Street	Sunday Street	91	1946
Caramel Way	Caramel Way	Webster Avenue	35	1949
	Hollace Street	Orbin Street	33	1940
Sorrell Street	Overcliff Street		11	
A Street	Lamont Way	Morrison Street	19	1950
	Courtright Street	Wing Way	4	1950
	Gass Avenue	Leonora Street	4	
Transvaal Avenue	Lapish Road	Haller Street	49	1949
Farris Street	Farris Street	Brighton Road	42	1980
Lenox Street	Wilson Avenue	Lenox Street	15	1980
McKees Lane	Burgess Street	Perrysville Avenue	37	1980
Burgess Street	Perrysville Avenue	Osgood Street	70	1980
	Osgood Street		63	
Mayfield Street	Norwood Avenue	Mohn Way	42	1953
Delger Street	Hawkins Street	Delger Street	25	1980
	Perrysville Avenue	Oak Park Road	39	1960
Sigma Way	Watson Boulevard	Delaware Street	74	1949
	Tretow Street	Watson Boulevard	3	
Santiago Street	Franklin	Santiago Street	11	1940
Woodsdale Way	Bascom Street	Perryview Avenue	41	1950

STREET NAME	FROM STREET	TO STREET	STEPS	YEAR
	Roosevelt Avenue	Bascom Street	23	1950
	Montview Street	Wabana Street	73	1949
Doak Way	Oakdale Street	Dornestic Street	168	1940
Groyne Street	Groyne Street	end	34	1950
Suffolk Street	East Street	Peekskill Street	97	
Bark Street	Wurzel Avenue		76	
Bly Street	Royal Street	end	48	1949
Langraf Street	Mina Street	Shine Way	28	1983
	Warren Street		22	1990
Lanark Street	Catona Street	Hargate Way	19	
Cemetery Avenue	Morris Avenue	Meadville Street	7	1980
McNaughter Street	Olive Street	Mountford Avenue	23	
McNaughter Street	Olive Street		12	1950
Walz Road	Walz Road	Rhinne Street	4	
	Letsche Street	Olive Street	165	1950
	Glenside Street	Roosevelt Avenue	76	1950
Flora Street	Transvaal Avenue	Winter Alley	48	1980
	Rostock Street	Solar Street	92	1946
	Girdley Way	Staab Street	35	1949
Litchfield Street	Chartiers Avenue	Toledo Street	113	1947
Universal Street	Chartiers Avenue	Newcomer Street	60	1950
Adon Street	Chartiers Avenue	Huxley Street	62	1947

STREET NAME	FROM STREET	TO STREET	STEPS	YEAR
Huxley Street	Chartiers Avenue	Adon Street	56	1949
Mutual Street	Chartiers Avenue	Mutual Street	37	1950
Pritchard Street	Chartiers Avenue	Kelvin Street	41	1948
Isabella Street	Oltman Street	Chartiers Avenue	81	1949
Mutual Street	Mutual Street	Kelvin Street	36	
Jeffers Street	Faronia Street	Middletown Road	76	1946
Fadette Street	Petty Way	Pritchard Street	51	1980
Straka Street	Berry Street	Sanborn Street	104	
Thornton Street	Surban Street	Sherwood Avenue	41	1960
	Chartiers Avenue	Tyndall Street	32	1982
Radcliffe Street	Maple Way	Stadium Street	22	1980
Radcliffe Street	Stadium Street	Strickler Street	64	1950
	W Carson Street		32	1949
Wyckoff Street	Merwyn Avenue	Stafford Street	83	1949
	Narcissus Avenue	Hammond Street	114	1951
Ashlyn Street	Stafford Street	Brevet Way	102	1952
Boulder Way	Stafford Street	Glen Mawr	138	1947
Merwyn Avenue	Ashlyn Street	Merwyn Avenue	4	1952
Fairdale Street	Adon Street	Jean Street	108	1948
Tybee Street	Universal Street	Tybee Street	21	1980
	Emporia Street	Tybee Street	12	1960
	India Street	Dickens Street	12	1940

STREET NAME	FROM STREET	TO STREET	STEPS	YEAR
Thayer Street	Tuxedo Street	Thayer Street	51	1970
Jenkins Street	Berry Street	Jenkins Street	16	1950
Round Top Street	Arnold Street	Norwalk Street	53	1948
Irvona Way	Clairtonica Street		41	
Ridenour Avenue	Earlham Street	end	107	1980
	Crotzer Street	Sedley Way	66	
Milnor Street	Clearview Avenue	Barr Avenue	75	
Milnor Street	Barr Avenue	Attal Way	46	
	Crafton Boulevard	Clearview Avenue	31	1990
Clairhaven Street	Arnold Street	Norwalk Street	67	1945
Balfour Street	Steuben Street	Lander Street	232	1947
Planet Street	Elliott Street	Attica Street	133	1947
	Violet Way	Steuben Street	31	1960
Lorentz Avenue	Steuben Street	Harker Street	88	1990
Small Way	Crucible Street	Dickens Street	117	1949
	Crafton Boulevard	Clearview Avenue	18	1990
	Attal Way	Rydall Street	51	1947
Dale Street	Noblestown Road	Code Way	43	1980
	Noblestown Road	Guyland Street	45	1980
	Baldwick Road	Noblestown Road	11	1980
Oakwood Drive	Glendon Street	Oakwood Drive	28	1948
	Oakwood Drive	Balver Avenue	18	1964

STREET NAME	FROM STREET	TO STREET	STEPS	YEAR
Kerr Street	South Main Street	Walbridge Street	7	
	Walbridge Street	McDade Way	199	1985
	Walbridge Street		3	1985
Elbon Way	Harker Street	Herschel Street	216	1947
	Steuben Street	Crucible Street	67	1949
Amherst Street	Chartiers Avenue	Janewood Way	53	
Fairview Street	Furley Street	Uvilla Street	101	1947
	Steuben Street	Attica Street	90	1947
	Attica Street	Furley Street	3	
	Attica Street	Herndon Street	7	1947
Valonia Street	Attica Street	Advent Street	187	1945
	Plover Way	Valonia Street	16	
	Lorentz Avenue	Navajo Way	7	
	Paranassus Way	Marlow Street	67	
	Paranassus Way	Comstock Way	22	
Ryan Street	South Main Street	Steuben Street	48	1941
Endness Street	Woodville Avenue	Corinth Street	42	
	Corinth Street	Journal Street	?	
	Journal Street	Corinth Street	64	
	323 Milroy Street	301 Milroy Street	26	1980
	Bothwell Street	Viola Street	8	
	Magnet Street	Brule Street	32	

STREET NAME	FROM STREET	TO STREET	STEPS	YEAR
Anise Way	Banksville Avenue	Trippet Avenue	77	1948
	Woodcove Place	Kirsopp Avenue	73	1958
	Banksville Avenue	Carnahan Road	74	
	Banksville Avenue	Louisiana Avenue	90	1964
Louisiana Avenue	Ordinance Street	Wenzel Avenue	141	1950
Neeld Way	Wenzel Avenue	Candace Street	81	1951
	Candace Street	Broadway Avenue	8	1950
Candace Street	Crosby Avenue	Shiras Avenue	56	1950
	Hillgrove Avenue		59	1980
	Banksville Road	Strachan Avenue	98	1964
	Greentree Road	Ridgemont Drive	12	
	Shaler Street	Clarence Street	19	1950
	Clarence Street	Edith Street	19	1950
Greenleaf Street	Shaler Street	Seward Street	74	1980
	Clarence Street	Orlena Way	15	
	Edith Street	Augusta Street	72	1950
	Seward Street	Republic Street	17	1950
		Greenleaf Street	26	
Well Street	Plymouth Street	Oneida Street	81	1988
Virginia Street	Sweetbriar Street	Plymouth Street	96	1950
	Merrimac Street	LaBelle Street	64	1946
	Merrimac Street	Omaha Street	23	1960

STREET NAME	FROM STREET	TO STREET	STEPS	YEAR
	Sewer Way	Redoak Way	6	1980
	Hallock Street	Meridan Street	47	1990
Pawnee Street	Oneida Street	Cohasset Street	52	1990
Sioux Way	Sioux Way	Pawnee Street	8	1990
	Plymouth Street	Oneida Street	50	1990
	Merrimac Street	Bertha Street	56	1946
	end	Wyoming Street	133	1952
Vinecliffe Street	East Sycamore Street	Vinecliffe Street	75	1952
	East Sycamore Street	Wyoming Street	5	
	Virginia Avenue	Natchez Street	81	1980
Luxbridge Way	Luxbridge Way	Vinecliffe Street	12	
	Leipsic Way	Natchez Street	13	
Halpin Street	Balonda Street	Leipsic Way	136	1952
	Gray Street	Dilworth Street	23	
	Gray Street	Cowan Street	18	1980
	Southern Avenue	Boggs Avenue	35	1982
	Norton Street	Dilworth Street	33	1951
	Southern Avenue	Greenbush Street	43	1950
	Griffin Street	Burson Way	29	1988
Dewitt Street	Southern Avenue	Griffin Street	33	1975
	end	Ruth Street	12	1950
	Westwood Street	Ruth Street	58	1997

STREET NAME	FROM STREET	TO STREET	STEPS	YEAR
Eureka Street	Habermann Avenue	Laclede Street	29	1980
	Cushman Street		21	1980
Mann Street	Woodruff Street	Rubicon Street	107	1938
Mann Street	Rubicon Street	Grace Street	42	1938
Mann Street	Grace Street	Belonda Street	83	1980
	Virginia Avenue	Shiloh Street	8	1938
	Kathleen Street	Kambach Street	22	1990
Ottawa Street	Penelope Street	Southern Avenue	59	1951
Harwood Way	Busway	Secane Avenue	21	1949
	Pasadena Street	Allepo Way	8	
	Allepo Way	Estella Avenue	32	
	Beltzhoover Avenue	end	45	
Eureka Street	East Warrington Avenue	Industry Street	19	
	Industry Street	Climax Street	26	1940
	Nina Way	Loyal Way	120	
Montooth Street	West Warrington Avenue	Nina Way	37	1988
Laverne Street	West Warrington Avenue	Nina Way	60	1990
	Nina Way	Climax Street	19	1950
Habermann Avenue	Loyal Way	Freeland Street	40	1990

STREET NAME	FROM STREET	TO STREET	STEPS	YEAR
Delmont Avenue	Loyal Way	Freeland Street	59	1948
	Lehr Way	Cedarhurst Street	7	
Habermann Avenue	Chalfont Street	Orient Way	12	
	Orient Way	Sylvania Street	6	
Bernd Street	Zelda Way	Althea Street	89	1988
	Zelda Way	Michigan Street	17	1988
	Mount Oliver Street	Arlington Avenue	35	1960
Cedarhurst Street	Arlington Avenue	Ibis Way	39	1953
	Arlington Avenue	Knox Avenue	17	1989
	Mount Oliver Street	Arlington Avenue	62	1990
	Mount Oliver Street	Breeze Way	7	
	Mount Oliver Street	Arlington Avenue	49	1970
	Brossville Street	Arlington Avenue	7	
	Arlington Avenue		8	
Marengo Street	Arlington Avenue	Eccles Street	46	1948
	Spring Street	Arlington Avenue	4	1990
Syrian Street	Arlington Avenue	Azul Street	103	1990
Arlington Avenue	Williams Street		64	1990
Weber Way	Weber Way	Rahe Street	3	
	Arlington Avenue	Waite Street	53	1970
	Arlington Avenue	Charcot Street	14	1990
Will Way	Arlington Avenue	Una Way	59	1950

STREET NAME	FROM STREET	TO STREET	STEPS	YEAR
Rinne Street	Arlington Avenue	Una Way	21	1950
	Azul Street	Bis Way	14	1949
	Ibis Way	Brownsville Road	15	1990
	Knox Avenue	Brownsville Road	49	1929
	Fordyce Street	Conniston Avenue	57	1947
Grimes Avenue	Kernel Way	Suncrest Street	34	
Georgia Avenue	Arabella Street	Moore Avenue	51	1948
	Bigger Street	Taft Avenue	12	
	Streetcar Line	Buffington Avenue	30	1990
	Streetcar Line	Boggston Avenue	42	1990
	Amanda Avenue	Brownsville Road	9	
	Weber Way	Waite Street		1996
	Knox Avenue	Brownsville Road	2	1996
Fisher Street	Otilla Street	Gorgas Street	14	1990
Rectenwald Street	Walde Street	Ignatius Way	29	1948
	Ignatius Way	Cathedral Avenue	37	1948
	Fisher Street	Ormsby Street	34	1990
Pliney Way	Mountain Street	Pliney Way	26	
Como Street	Saint Joseph Street	Ormsby Avenue	41	1953
	Mount Joseph Street	Oakhurst Way	29	1949
	Oakhurst Way	Brownsville Road	167	1949
	Westmont Avenue	Brownsville Road	24	1949

STREET NAME	FROM STREET	TO STREET	STEPS	YEAR
East Cherryhill Street	Amanda Street	Brownsville Road	60	1949
	Concordia Street	Amanda Street	31	1949
Leolyn Street	South Way	E. Meyers Street	57	1948
Highnote Way	Anglo Way	The Boulevard	125	1972
Highnote Way	Alries Street	Romance Street	74	1950
	Alries Street	South Way	14	1970
	Fromm Way	Hazeldell Street	61	1970
	Revision Way	Hornaday Road	21	
Redrose Avenue	Madeline Street	Redrose Avenue	35	1946
Custer Avenue	Brinwood Avenue	Kirk Avenue	101	1964
	Carrick Avenue	Lauch Way	8	
Sanderson Avenue	Matilda Street	Merrit Avenue	87	1952
Ravilla Avenue	Almont Street	Valera Avenue	55	1948
Mosgrove Street	Nobles Lane	Cloverdale Street	62	1973
Hawridge Way	Denise Street	Nobles Lane	22	1980
Glade Street	Nobles Lane	Cloverdale Street	59	1948
Dartmore Street	Englert Street	Dartmore Street	8	
Sinton Way	Dartmore Street	Lucina Street	221	1945
Englert Street	Dartmore Street	Fairland Street	92	1948
Antenor Way	Maytide Street	Antenor Avenue	101	1949
	Glenbury Street	Pinecastle Avenue	55	1947

STREET NAME	FROM STREET	TO STREET	STEPS	YEAR
Fan Street	Glenbury Street	Seldon Place	79	1949
Vineland Street	Aaron Avenue	Vineland Street	38	1990
Jacob Street	Brookline Boulevard	Sunbeam Way	364	1988
	Hillview Street	Kingwood Street	95	1950
Hillview Street	Kingwood Street	Homehurst Street	111	1949
	Glenhurst Road	Lougean Avenue	77	1953
Oakleaf Drive	Leaside Drive	Oakleaf Drive	46	1948
	Mifflin Road	Cox Place	65	1960
Kinley Avenue	Lindberg Avenue	Barberry Street	42	1965
	Oakleaf Drive	Interboro Avenue	18	1960
	Overbrook Boulevard	Dartmore Street	12	1994
	Saw Mill Run	Busway	13	
	Ansonia Place	Saw Mill Run	36	
	Ansonia Place	Saw Mill Run	12	
	Ansonia Place	Mobile Home Court	32	
Paradox Way	Rutherford Avenue	Beechview Avenue	158	1950
	Goldstrom Avenue	Hampshire Avenue	99	1951
	Coast Avenue	Rutherford Avenue	73	1950
Rutherford Avenue	Rutherford Avenue	Broadway Avenue	50	1950
	Belasco Avenue	Broadway Avenue	86	
	Coast Avenue	Cagwin Street	80	
Belasco Avenue	Cagwin Street	Broadway Avenue	93	1951

STREET NAME	FROM STREET	TO STREET	STEPS	YEAR
Fitzhugh Way	Jillson Street	Broadway Avenue	76	1980
	Kenilworth Street	Brookline Boulevard	9	
	Kenilworth Street	Plainview Avenue	5	
Kenilworth Street	Bodkin Street	Brookline Boulevard	20	1952
Bodkin Street	Amman Street	Brookline Boulevard	21	1952
	West Liberty Avenue	Waddington Avenue	26	1952
Stapleton Street	West Liberty Avenue	Amman Street	47	1952
Templeton Street	West Liberty Avenue	Plainview Avenue	190	1951
Peola Road	West Liberty Avenue	Texdale Street	116	1945
Belle Isle Avenue	Woodward Avenue	Woodward Avenue	60	
Belle Isle Avenue	Plainview Avenue	Plainview Avenue	14	1947
Belle Isle Avenue	West Liberty Avenue	Dabney Way	71	1954
Ray Avenue	West Liberty Avenue	Pioneer Avenue	378	1950
Stetson Street	Wellington Way	Woodward Avenue	64	1997
Clover Street	McKean Street	Cobden Street	42	1931
South 4th Street	Canton Avenue	East Carson Street	56	
Hampshire Avenue	Graymore Street	Napoleon Street	58	1950
Hampshire Avenue	Coast Avenue	Canton Avenue	112	
Canton Avenue	Goldstrom Avenue	Hampshire Avenue	54	1970
Alverado Avenue	Goldstrom Avenue	Alverado Avenue	76	1951
Belasco Avenue	Napoleon Street	Belasco Avenue	12	1950
Bayonne Avenue	Napoleon Street	Alverado Avenue	95	

STREET NAME	FROM STREET	TO STREET	STEPS	YEAR
Andick Way	Tropical Avenue	Gladys Avenue	11	1964
	Kenberma	Dagmar Avenue	2	
	Dagmar Avenue	Fallowfield Avenue	76	1952
Kiralfy Avenue	Kiralfy Avenue	Tonopah Avenue	73	1950
Coast Avenue	Dagmar Avenue	Fallowfield Avenue	101	1952
Dagmar Avenue	Tonopah Avenue	Alturia Avenue	44	1950
Fairacres Avenue	Colebrook Avenue	Tonopah Avenue	63	1950
	Colebrook Avenue	Ringwalt Avenue	38	1950
Tonopah Avenue	Westinghouse Avenue	Ringwalt Avenue	32	1950
Crosby Avenue	Crosby Avenue	Brookline Boulevard	19	1940
Kenilworth Street	Brookline Boulevard	Aldyl Avenue	52	1951
Waltham Street	Dawn Avenue	Charm Avenue	26	1950
Ballinger Street	Edgebrook Avenue	Herber Way	167	1948
Edgebrook Avenue	Belair Avenue	Brookline Boulevard	26	
Stebbins Street	Harex Way	Bay Ridge Avenue	38	1938
Repeal Way	Glenarm Avenue	Gallion Avenue	45	1950
Wedgemere Place	Gallion Avenue	Raeburn Way	24	
Stetson Street	Woodward Avenue	Lapeer Way	54	1950
Stetson Street	Lapeer Way	Pioneer Avenue	24	1950
Napoleon Street	Goldstrom Avenue	Bayonne Avenue	113	1974
Graymore Street	Coast Avenue	Hampshire Avenue	35	1951
Ordinance Avenue	Louisiana Avenue	Connecticut Avenue	109	1950

STREET NAME	FROM STREET	TO STREET	STEPS	YEAR
Crimson Avenue	Traymore Avenue	Sebring Avenue	51	1950
	Suburban Avenue	Traymore Avenue	72	1950
Hobson Street	Breining Street	Hobson Street	18	1980
Colmar Street	Blessing Street	Bernhardt Way	73	
Bernhardt Way	Harry Street	Webster Street	11	1950
	Negley Run Boulevard	Leonora Street	?	
Andick Way	Westfield Street	Rockland Avenue	38	1960
Eldridge Street	Forward Avenue	Eldridge Street	4	
Chartiers Avenue	Danley Street	Praego Street	18	
Chartiers Avenue	Azalea Street		14	
Wabash Street	Wabash Street	Steuben Street	6	
Dartmore Street	Saw Mill Run	Sinton Avenue	25	
Horning Street	Ivyglen Street	Lodge Street	46	
Saint Norberts Street	Ivyglen Street		10	
Lodge Street	Ivyglen Street	Dead end	15	
Rosetta Street	North Pacific Avenue	Monroe Street	22	
Hancock Street	Ridgway Street	Beelen Street	66	
Kirkpatrick Street	Kirkpatrick Street	Gregory Street	5	
	Pius Street		18	
	near Stockholm Street	Bigelow Boulevard (park)	65	
Rutherford Avenue	Rutherford Avenue		29	

STREET NAME	FROM STREET	TO STREET	STEPS	YEAR
56th Street	Celadine Street	Alford Way	8	1940
56th Street	Wycliff Street	Celadine Street	119	1946
56th Street	Duncan Street	Wycliff Street	26	
	Juno Street	Boulevard of the Allies	73	
	Second Avenue	Bohem Street	277	
South 15th Street	Clinton Street	Pius Street	32	
South 15th Street	South 15th Street	Clinton Street	120	
Hartford Street	Hartford Street	Hartford Street	20	
	McCartney Street	Noblestown Road	115	
Dengler Street	Arlington Avenue	Dengler Street	14	
Edgerton Avenue	Hastings Street	South Linden Avenue	27	
Federal Hill Avenue	Saline Street	Luwick Street	8	
	Luella Street	Heim Street	75	1950
Sunapee Way	Maeburn Road	Shady Avenue	30	
Milo Street	Cape May Avenue	Suburban Avenue	96	2002
Yew Street	Gross Street	Yew Street	30	
	Loretta Street	Exeter Street	72	
	Melbourne Street	Millington Street	11	
Granite Street	Crockett Way	Orbin Street	26	
	Orbin Street	Orbin Street	20	
	Kirk Street	Spencer Street	25	
	Catoctin Street	Watson Street	48	

STREET NAME	FROM STREET	TO STREET	STEPS	YEAR
Complete Street	Embury Street	Rancheria Street	24	
Winnhurst Street	Complete Street	Geyer Avenue	63	
Zara Street	Winnhurst Street	Brighton Avenue	10	
Soffel Street	Zara Street	Belzhoover Avenue	12	
	Southern Street	Lena Street	38	
	Lelia Street	Albert Street	25	
	Kearsage Street	end	30	
Moyer Street	Moyer Street	Chartiers Avenue	50	
	Zephyr Avenue	Glenmar Street	5	
Meyers Street	Meyers Street	Mount Joseph Street	10	
Redrose Street	Poplar Grove Street	Plummet Street	19	
	Woodbourne Street	Bay Ridge Street	20	
	Fordham Street	Taxola Street	6	
	Bellair Street	Dahlia Street	21	
	Pringle Street	Pringle Street	29	
	Pringle Street		23	
Glendon Street	Grassmere Street	Pennsdale Street	72	
	Flatbush Street		22	
	Gagwin Way		15	
Coyne Street	Coyne Street	Winterburn Street	18	
Ardary Street	Columbo Street		21	

APPENDIX B

How the Sad Steps
Helped Save Our Steps

Every day Lizbeth walked to school down her very own set of city steps. Well they weren't hers, exactly, but she had used these steps so many times that she thought of them as her own. These were special steps, though. In fact, they were really a street named Spring Street. Her father had told her that only in Pittsburgh can you find streets that are steps (or steps that are streets).

In the past few days, though, Lizbeth thought her favorite steps seemed sad. They had pieces missing and the handrails were rusty. She wondered how she could help fix the steps and make them happy and healthy again.

She told her father about the steps, and he walked with her to see. He saw that the steps were broken in places and the handrail loose in spots. He said, "Lizzie, I don't think the steps are sad. I think they may not be safe." Lizbeth was surprised and asked what they could do. Her father said that he would talk to the city and see if they could fix them.

The next day her father went to City Hall to talk about the steps. He was surprised to learn that Lizbeth's steps were not alone. There were hundreds of sets of city steps in the city and many needed to be fixed. The man at City Hall said that there were a lot of other things in the city that needed to be fixed and they could not fix the steps.

Lizbeth was surprised to hear that there were many other sets of sad steps and that the city would not fix her steps. When she next walked to school down her sad steps she thought that there must be a way to make her steps happy again. When she got to school she talked to her teacher about her sad steps and to her friends during recess.

After recess the teacher thought the students looked worried about something. She asked what was wrong and was surprised to hear that they were all worried about the steps. So, they all talked about what they could do. They talked and thought and then talked and thought some more. Finally, Mary Louise said, "Let's start a program to save the steps. We could call it Save Our Steps."

"Wow," everyone said. "That's great!"

The teacher agreed and said she would talk to the art teacher about making a sign.

Later that week, the teacher showed them the sign the art teacher had made and gave everyone a copy. All were excited and then talked and thought again about how the program would work.

When Lizbeth showed her father the Save Our Steps sign and said they were planning a program, he said, "Wonderful." Then he said that he would have some Save Our Steps tee-shirts and buttons made for them.

Wow, thought Lizbeth. *This could be exciting.*

What joy there was in the classroom when Lizbeth brought in the shirts and buttons. Before long the whole class and the teacher were wearing the Save Our Steps shirts and buttons. When they went out to play at recess the other classes were asking questions and soon wanting to join the Save Our Steps program.

When the students in all the classes had the Save Our Steps shirts and buttons, the principal was pleased and said that they would have a Save Our Steps Day every Friday. So it was that every Friday all the students wore their Save Our Steps shirts and buttons and talked about the city steps in class.

Soon people started to notice the shirts and buttons on the boys and girls and asked about them. Before long more and more people got interested in the steps and children from other schools asked if they could join the Save Our Steps program.

It was only several months later that every school had a Save Our Steps program on Fridays and all the school children wore their Save Our Steps shirts and buttons.

Stories and pictures about the program started to appear in the newspapers and on the news programs. Then one Saturday a lot of grown-ups and children got together at Lizbeth's sad steps and started to paint and fix them.

"No, no, no!" the men from the city said. "Those are our steps and only we can fix them."

"Then fix them," the people said.

The next week almost all the people in the city asked that the steps be fixed. The city had no choice but to agree to fix them all.

Now, when Lizbeth walks down *her* set of city steps she sees that they are all fixed and painted and look like new. They are now happy and healthy, as are all the steps in Pittsburgh!

About the Author

Bob Regan is retired and lives in Pittsburgh where he pretends to be a native.

About the Photographer

Jeff Wingard, Creative Imagery, LLC, has been passionate about photography since childhood.